And Then
I Had
Teenagers

Books by the Yates Family

And Then
I Had
Teenagers

Susan Alexander Yates

© 2001 by Susan Alexander Yates

Published by Revell
a division of Baker Publishing Group
P.O. Box 6287, Grand Rapids, MI 49516-6287
www.revellbooks.com

Spire edition published 2010
ISBN 978-0-8007-8791-2

Printed in the United States of America

Scripture is taken from the HOLY BIBLE, NEW INTERNATIONAL VERSION®.
NIV®. Copyright © 1973, 1978, 1984 by International Bible Society. Used by
permission of Zondervan. All rights reserved.

10   11   12   13   14   15   16   7   6   5   4   3   2   1

With thanksgiving for my husband
Johnny

our eight treasures and teachers
Allison & Will
John & Alysia
Chris & Christy
Susy
Libby

and with gratitude for two new treasures
Scott
McLean

Contents

Contents

Acknowledgments

Writing a book can be a lonely adventure. It makes you really appreciate friends and family who encourage you and pray for you. I am most grateful to my husband, Johnny, and especially to my *almost* ten kids! Allison and Will Gaskins (Allison's husband), John and Alysia Ponzi Yates (John's wife), Chris and Christy Borgman Yates (Chris's wife), and Susy (and fiancé, Scott Anderson) and Libby (and fiancé, McLean Wilson). They give me ideas, let me tell stories about them, and pray faithfully for me. My mother, Fran Alexander, and mother-in-law, Sue Tucker Yates, have been my role models. When I grow up, I want to be just like them.

Many friends have prayed for me and encouraged me along the way. I'm thankful for Ann Holladay, Brenda Hunter, Becky Pippert (Molenhouse), Gail Nolan, Holly Leachman, Debbie Sweek, Sarah Dow Reimers, Christin McGovern, Anne Cregger, Jane Eboch, Kim Doerr, Tucker Viccellio, Priscilla Reimers, Judy Thomsen, Molly Shafferman, Julia Mitchell, Cary Umhau, Esther Powell, Betsy Roadman, Georgia Brennecke, Ann Hibbard, Beth Spring, Elaine Metcalf, and Heidi Metcalf.

My sister, Fran Cade, and the "Birmingham Moms" gave me a fun weekend away, with many wonderful insights. Thank you for sharing your lives with me!

I am especially grateful for all the parents who shared their stories with me. Many are friends at The Falls Church (Episcopal), where we have served for twenty-two years. All of the stories in the book are true; however, in many cases the names have been changed to protect an individual's privacy.

A very special word of thanks goes to Missy Eboch, Christie Schweer, Mac Rogers, Rob Gaskins, and each of their parents. These friends have graciously permitted me to tell their difficult stories (in chapter 9) with the hope that they will be an encouragement to you. These families are available as a resource to you. You may contact them through me at Baker Publishing Group.

Allison, my daughter, my friend, and coauthor on several projects, has edited this manuscript in the midst of moving and chasing our two precious grandchildren, Caroline, three years old, and Will Jr., one! How blessed I am to have her. Our neighbors Bill and Susan Buckingham have kept my computer behaving and have been patient with my ineptitude. It's been a pleasure to work with Stephen Griffith, my agent, and the wonderful team at Baker.

Thanks be to God for these and many others who have walked alongside me in this project. Most especially, I am thankful to God. He is faithful.

> For his compassions never fail.
> They are new every morning;
>   great is your faithfulness.
>
> Lamentations 3:22–23

Introduction

At the Window

Standing at my front window, I watched for the familiar blonde head to appear. And I braced myself for what was about to happen. Slumped shoulders and a lowered head might mean trouble, whereas a light skip with a swinging backpack could mean a pleasant greeting was in store.

What will she be like today? I mused. *Will she be on a high because she was asked to sit with the "right girls" at lunch, or will she be in an irritable funk because a certain boy didn't speak to her in the hall?*

I had no way of knowing. I had a fourteen-year-old.

And then she was home.

"Hi, honey," I greeted her, opening the front door. "How was your day?"

"Okay," she replied in an exasperated voice as she threw her backpack on the floor.

Making a beeline for the kitchen, she bumped into her younger brother.

"Why don't you look where you're going?" she barked.

Casting a quick glance into the refrigerator, she turned accusingly to me.

"Why don't we ever have any good food to eat in this house, anyway?"

Not waiting for an answer, she stomped out and headed into her room, slamming the door with a loud bang that seemed to say, *So there, it's all your fault!*

As I stood in silence, my son looked at me with a puzzled expression.

"Mom, what's the matter with her?" he asked.

"*Adolescence*, that's what," I sighed.

It didn't *seem* that long since I'd stood at the same window, waiting for my husband to come to my rescue. *Then* I was blocking out the cries of fifteen-month-old twins with ear infections, ignoring the war taking place between our four- and six-year-old boys, and not even caring where our eight-year-old was. *Then* I watched for HIS car to turn in the driveway. With coat and purse in hand, I greeted him at the door.

"Hi, honey. You've heard of runaway kids—well, I'm a runaway mom. They're *all* fussing. They're *all yours*. I'll be back in about three hours, when I'm sure *you* will have them *all* asleep."

Then I had five kids, ages eight and under, and I ran away. But *now* I'd become a parent of five teens and preteens. And I'm not supposed to run away. It's immature.

Allison was nineteen, John seventeen, Chris fifteen, and our twins, Susy and Libby, about to turn thirteen. We had a house full of hormones. And we knew that life with teens was different than life with toddlers.

12

Back then we couldn't get them to sleep. *Now* we can't get them up.

Then we used to be up at night feeding babies. *Now* we're up at night waiting for them to come in.

Then they didn't care if their shorts were clean. *Now* they have to wear shorts that aren't too clean and that are made of perfectly faded denim.

Then they wanted us to understand their baby coos. *Now* they talk to each other in Spanish so we can't understand.

Then we couldn't get them to take a shower. *Now* we can't get them out of the bathroom.

Then we never could find a lost toddler's shoe when we needed it. *Now* we trip over Chris's size 13 shoes.

Then we used to worry about what the kids wore. *Now* Chris looks at his younger sisters and says, "*I'd* never let *my* girls go to school dressed like that!"

Then the kids used to promise us they "could be responsible." *Now* John says, "It's a pain being responsible."

Then we used to be embarrassed when they acted foolishly. *Now* John says, "My girl's coming over in a minute, Mom. Don't act like a grown-up fool!"

Then we used to go see *Bambi* and cry. *Now* we watch *Father of the Bride* and cry.

So many changes. So many challenges, so many fears. If your kids are approaching the teen years, you are scared. If they are in the middle of them, you are overwhelmed. And if they are in the later teen years, you wonder, *Is it already too late?*

You may have a nineteen-year-old daughter who's been a compliant, easy teen to raise, but now you are teetering on the brink of major rebellion with your thirteen-year-old son. How can two teens in the same family be so different? You may be a single parent, and with no partner to discuss things with, you feel very much alone. Or you may have kids on the verge of the teen years, and because of your own "sordid" background, you wonder if your kids have a chance.

As we've gone through the teen years with our five and talked to many other parents and teens, we've found great comfort in knowing there are others experiencing the same challenges.

Challenges, yes. But many blessings as well. Turn the page and join in as we take an honest look at our lives together and discover some practical ways to enable this season to be not merely endured, but also *enjoyed*.

In chapter 1 we will take a look at ten of the common challenges facing parents of teenagers. The subsequent chapters will deal with each challenge in greater detail. We will talk honestly and practically about each challenge, yet we will also focus on the tremendous blessings to be found during these teen years. As you read, resist the temptation to flip to the "Hot Topics" chapter for a quick solution to your situation. There are no quick solutions, no simple answers in raising teens. You cannot compartmentalize a teenager, and each situation involves a wonderfully complicated child of God *and* his or her complex parents. How you handle the issues will depend upon the relationships you are establishing with your kids. It's never too late to improve a relationship.

1

The Fearful Parent

Help, what if they . . . ? What if I . . . ?

We were sitting at the local Starbucks sipping hot cups of special coffees and talking about our kids. Each of us was in various stages of raising teenagers. One had a twelve-year-old son, another a nineteen-year-old daughter. One had two step-teens, and another was a single mom. As we chatted, several other moms pulled up chairs to join in the conversation.

"When you think of raising teens, what's your main emotional response?" I asked.

"FEAR," one mom immediately responded, and others quickly agreed.

"I want my daughter to make wise choices, and I'm so afraid that she won't. Oh, I know she'll make mistakes, but I'm afraid her poor choices might harm her or someone else for life," one mom said anxiously.

"I'm frustrated," added another mom. "I'm the controlling type, but now I sense I'm losing control. My son always has to have the last word. And he makes me feel so stupid."

"I've made so many mistakes as a stepmother, I'm afraid that my stepdaughter will never forgive me," chimed in Cary, as tears began to trickle down her cheeks.

"I'm feeling lonely," confessed Beth. "My daughter and I have always been so close, but now she seems to be pulling away. She doesn't confide in me the way she used to. She wants privacy. She tells her friends things instead of me."

"I was a rebellious hell-raiser, and I'm so afraid my daughter will do what I did. Even though I know I'm forgiven, I still experience such sadness for the pain I caused my parents, and I still carry painful scars myself," Shelly lamented.

"My son is eighteen and uncommunicative. He doesn't want to have anything to do with church or youth group. He's hanging out with kids I don't like, and I'm scared. I feel like we've lost him," another mom commented.

"I have a good relationship with my two teens," said one mom who seemed uncomfortable. "But everyone keeps saying, 'You just wait until . . .' So now I feel anxious because I'm *not* having problems. And I'm confused. Do the teen years have to be awful?"

Fear, frustration, guilt, loneliness, confusion.
And those *What ifs*.
What if I've already messed up my kid? *What if* she turns out like me? *What if* he rejects God? *What if* he gets into drugs? *What if . . . ?*

It is a scary time. A lonely time. A confusing time. We may have fears we're afraid to admit. We may have unresolved issues from our own past that are rearing their ugly heads. There may be tension in our marriage over how best to handle a teen. Or we may be single parents feeling very lonely.

When we realize, *I'm not the only one who feels like this*, we will be comforted.

Having raised five teens and having talked with numerous other parents of teens, my husband, Johnny, and I have come to see that there are many common challenges we all encounter as parents in this new season. Articulating these challenges can be encouraging because it helps us realize that someone else is dealing with the same issues we are. It can be refreshing to talk through these issues and discover that many of them have practical solutions.

Finally, these challenges and issues can help us become people of deeper faith. We can experience God's hand in our lives in an even more profound way as we all, parents and teens alike, grow through our children's teen years.

In the next few pages we will identify ten common challenges of raising teenagers. Each chapter that follows will highlight one of these issues and suggest practical solutions. At the end of each chapter you will find focus questions you can use to enhance your study. You can benefit greatly if you use this book in a group study, allowing these focus questions to become a springboard for discussion.

A Quick Look at Ten Common Challenges

What's Normal, What's Not?

"How was your day?" I asked my son John, who was seated at the kitchen table for an after-school snack.

"Fine." Period. Silence.

"Anything interesting happen today?" I continued.

"Oh, Mother, I feel like I'm at an inquisition. You're so nosy," he remarked as he grabbed his books and headed to his room.

Again, my once talkative, affectionate, fun-loving son had shut me out. At thirteen he expressed himself by acting ultracool and uncommunicative. He wasn't much fun to be with, and he certainly did not seem to enjoy my presence. *Why,* I wondered, *do I even make the effort to be here when he comes home from school? It doesn't seem to make any difference to him. Is his behavior normal? Is it a stage? Will it pass? Am I overreacting? How should I handle this?*

Everything I thought I knew about parenting flew out the window when our first child hit the teen years. I seemed to have had answers for toddlers, but for teens I didn't. At least with toddlers I had a sense of what is "normal." I knew most would rebel at having to go to bed, most would bite, most would not want to pick up toys, most would whine, most would defy. It was an easier time because I had a sense of what was to come, and I could plan. But it's not so easy with teens. Hormones, personality, and gender can combine to make the most experienced parents feel like fools. Just because our first teen responded in a certain way, there was no guarantee the next one would.

What *is* normal during this season? Why do different kids respond so differently? How do we discern what is a normal teenage problem and what is a genuine concern? How should we handle a particular child? What do we do about our own feelings of inadequacy? How can we parent our teen with confidence instead of fear?

Walking on Eggshells?

We were trying to have a nice family dinner—good conversation, encouraging words, lots of laughter. After all, that's what strong, happy, loving families do, don't they? Only it wasn't working in our house.

Allison, at fourteen, was in a funk. Nothing had gone right in her day. She didn't like the dinner I'd fixed. She didn't approve of my outfit. She especially didn't think her younger brothers were at all funny. And she absolutely did not want to talk. She just wanted to sulk and pout. No one wanted to talk to her either. That would just be asking for it. We felt like we were tiptoeing around a huge snake that might bite at any moment. Conversation became forced. We finished eating as soon as we could. It was not a warm, cozy picture of a loving Christian family.

What is going on? I asked myself. *My family is being held hostage by the roller-coaster moods of a self-centered teenager.*

It is not a fun place to be. How should we handle this? Do we ride it out or confront it head on? Who is controlling the atmosphere in our home? Is it our moody teen or her parents? How can we provide an encouraging atmosphere in our home during the turbulent teen years?

You Just Don't Understand!

Amy, seventeen, was in another verbal battle with her mom. She'd lied about where she'd been last night, and her mom had found out. Once again they stood eyeball-to-eyeball.

Amy ranted, "You don't understand anything. I just wish you'd get out of my life!"

"God gave me the job of raising you," Amy's mother calmly responded.

"Then why aren't you doing a better job of it?" Amy quickly shot back.

Round and round went their conversation. There were no winners. Only casualties. And once more Amy's mom felt like a failure.

It was so easy to talk to our young children. We understood them. We could give straight answers. There wasn't a communication problem. They shared their secrets with us. But not anymore.

Now when we try to understand, they "don't want to talk about it." Too often we get a cold shoulder, evasive answers, or just plain personal criticism. Our best friend may have a child that tells her everything, and since ours doesn't, we feel like a bad mom.

Nearly every teen and every parent puts "Better Communication" at the top of their wish list for their relationships with each other. How do we communicate in such a turbulent season? How can we understand one another better? When do we push to communicate, and when do we give space? How do we grow closer instead of drifting apart? How do we adapt our communication styles in the midst of so much change?

Why Can't You Just Trust Me?

Nancy, thirteen, came running in breathless.

"Mom, there's a Halloween party at the community center. My new friend, Alice, and I are going to go as witches and wear black miniskirts. Then we get to have an after party at Alice's house with some other kids and watch horror movies."

"I don't think so," her mom responded.

"Why can't I go? Nothing will happen. Don't you trust me? You never let me do anything!"

Every issue with our teen seems to turn into a major debate. Things aren't as black-and-white now. Often their arguments are so much better than ours. It was so much simpler when they were two and just had a temper tantrum. Then *we* won the battle. Now *they* present logical arguments.

Are we really the strictest, most unreasonable parents in town? we ask ourselves. What are reasonable limits?

We need to be letting go, but how do we decide what to let go of? What are swing issues to let slide, and what are crucial issues to hold to? Our decisions become more complicated when our best friend doesn't agree with our parenting style. She thinks we're too strict—or not strict enough. And there doesn't seem to be one right way for Christians to respond. How do we set limits and let go of our children? How do we discern what is best for our unique child?

Help! How Should I Handle . . . ?

Sex, dating, curfews, drinking, drugs, grades, driving, money, TV, movies, the Internet, music. Help! Won't somebody please tell me how to handle all these "Hot Topics"?

Is there one right formula for protecting my kids? No. Is it possible to handle these issues and avoid conflict? No. Is there any parent who feels he or she has done an adequate job in all these areas? No. Do teens have to rebel? No.

There are no perfect formulas for raising teens because there are no perfect parents and no perfect kids. Even Joseph had a conflict with Jesus. When He was twelve, Jesus didn't show up where He was supposed to be and didn't let His parents know where He was! God Himself understands the challenges of raising teenagers. Even Jesus, the only perfect son, managed to perplex His parents.

As parents we feel woefully inadequate as we face the challenges of today. There are so many more BIG issues, so many more temptations. And many of the issues our kids face can have life-threatening ramifications. In our postmodern culture, we wonder if we are too backward, too conservative, or if we are buying into the standards of our excessive culture without even realizing it. We feel confused. We feel alone.

Our teens are more informed, more advanced technologically, overwhelmed with options, and under tremendous stress. We too have pressures. Pressure to provide financially, to succeed in a career, to care for aging or ill parents, to grow spiritually, to raise kids who turn out to be useful, responsible adults.

In the midst of all these challenges, how do we handle these "Hot Topics" with our teen? Can we have reasonable discussions together? How? Where do we find practical advice for real-life situations?

But All My Friends Get To . . .

"Mom, there's a big concert out at the fairgrounds Saturday night, and a bunch of us want to go. Can I take the car and drive everyone?"

"Honey, you've only had your license two weeks, and you know our policy on driving others in the car. You don't have enough experience yet. I'm sorry, but you cannot take the car."

"Annie's mom lets *her* drive anyone anywhere, and she just got her license last week. She even has her own car! All my friends get to drive wherever they want. No one else has your stupid rules. You're so unfair!"

Driving. Licenses. Highways. Cars. Any one of these words will strike fear in the heart of the sanest parent. We know the dangers involved. We read the papers, watch the news, and we know, *it could have been my child in that accident.*

For us it's primarily a safety issue; for our child it's a peer pressure issue. It's a right of passage. It signifies another step into the adult world.

It isn't just cars. It's parties, grades, money, extracurricular activities, and many other issues. And our child isn't the only one who feels peer pressure. We too feel it from other parents. Our best friend lets her daughter drive anywhere, but we don't. Are we being too restrictive? Is she being too lenient? How do we handle these pressures? Who is right? What is right for our child?

We want to build good relationships with our teen's friends and their parents. How do we do it? Does peer pressure always have to be negative? Can't it be positive? How?

I'm Not Sure I Believe . . .

"I'm so scared," my friend confided. "What if my son rejects the faith? What if he goes in another direction? He's seventeen now, and he's showing signs of disinterest. He doesn't want to go to the guys' Bible study. He doesn't like to hang out with the Christian kids anymore. He won't talk to me about what's going on inside his head. I've prayed for him since he was born. He accepted Christ when he was young, but now . . . ? I keep praying for him, but I'm frightened. Why doesn't God answer? Where is God in this?"

It's a season of questioning. Why should a teen believe what he has been taught? Will he embrace his parents' faith and make it his own? Tough questions—necessary questions. With few easy answers.

What can we do to prepare our teen for taking ownership of his faith? What do we do when he doesn't believe? How can we grow in our own faith during this season?

I Never Thought "It" Would Happen to Me

Alex had always been independent. He'd take what his folks said and then put his own twist on it. And he liked girls—a lot. In sixth grade his dad found him making out in the last row of the movie theater. By sixteen he was a popular boy, one all the "cool" girls wanted to date. His parents were strong believers and had talked with him about sexual purity. And his parents had clear, firm house rules that he knew. One was, "No members of the opposite sex allowed in the house if a parent is not home." His junior year he started hanging out with a very "hot" girl. Alex's mom prayed hard for her son. Often she prayed that if he was doing anything wrong, he'd get caught. One summer day she felt compelled to go home from her office immediately. When she walked in the front door, she noticed a girl's purse on the chair. Marching up to Alex's room, she found the door locked.

"Son," she called, "you need to come out right now."

When he appeared, she asked, "Is anyone in there with you?"

"No, Mom," he replied, completely flustered. "No one is here."

Not willing to be misled, Mom marched straight into the room and found the "hot" girl struggling to get her clothes back on.

Alex was demoralized. His folks were devastated. Their son had lied; he'd violated house rules. He'd gotten himself involved in a wrong relationship. There were guilt, shame, and endless questions. *How could we have prevented this?* his dad and mom wondered. *How did we let him get this far down the wrong path? How did we get here? We never thought something like this would happen to us.*

But it had, and now the family had to decide what to do. What should their response be? Could God redeem even this? Could He use it for good in their son's life and in theirs?

What is our worst fear? What do we do if our fears are realized? What if our child gets into drugs, runs away, has an accident, gets pregnant, rejects the faith? What if "it" happens to us?

How Am I Supposed to Know Which College or Which Job Is Right?

The subject of college was really on Mary's mind. A single parent, she felt a bit overwhelmed as her son, Jeff, got closer to graduation. *Am I pushing him too much or not enough?* she agonized. *It's such a big decision, and once again I have to handle this by myself. I wish I had a partner to help me make wise decisions. I feel like a one-armed paperhanger.*

When I try to talk to my son, he just changes the subject or he says he's not ready to talk about life after high school. I know the competition that's out there for the good schools. We have to talk about it. I need help!

Andrew, seventeen, was competitive and intense. By the beginning of his junior year in high school, he'd researched colleges on the Internet and was already "stressing" over the fifteen applications he had decided to fill out. A driven over-achiever, he was determined to pursue every possibility. In the process he became irritable, anxious, and depressed. While his parents applauded his initiative, they became concerned with his obsessiveness. "How can we support him and yet help relieve some of his stress?" they asked.

Alice came up to me at a conference where I had been speaking. "Susan," she said, "neither my husband nor I went to college. No one in my family has ever gone, so we haven't really expected our daughter to go, but now I'm wondering if she should consider it. She makes good grades in school, but I don't know how to go about this college idea. It's so foreign to me. How do I know if she should work or go to college? I want to do what's best for my daughter. How do I find out what that is?"

We all have so many questions. There are either too many possibilities or too few options. And our child is either not interested enough or way too stressed about the issue. Often we don't know how to go about making the decision.

How do we begin? When do we begin? How do we discern what is right for our unique child? What should we look for in a school, in a job? How do we walk through this important decision with our child? How involved should we be, and how much do we leave up to our teen?

Leaving—Is My Child Ready? Am I?

I was sitting with two young men, one twenty-five and one nineteen, in a corporate dining room with a publishing executive. The executive was a girlfriend of mine who'd graciously agreed to have lunch with these boys, specifically to talk to the older one about job possibilities. His young friend was just along for the experience.

I was surprised as I observed what began to take place. The older boy took very little initiative in the conversation. He did not ask any questions. He seemed to have very little knowledge of the company. He had a hard time looking the executive in the eye, and his lack of manners seemed to make him ill at ease. I felt sorry for him. His young friend, on the other hand, had read up on the company. He asked good, specific questions. He stood to seat the executive. He offered to get her more coffee. He was fully at ease and engaged in the conversation.

Wow, I thought to myself. *This young boy is more equipped to move into the world than is his older friend. His parents have obviously trained him well. How did they do it?*

Watching this scene, I asked myself how my son would have behaved in this situation. Would he have been able to carry the conversation? Would he have had good manners? Would he know how to make those around him feel at ease?

This incident caused me to ask other questions as well: Am I equipping my child for living in the world? What other things does he need to know before he goes? Are there life skills that I should intentionally teach him? What are they? How do I do it and when do I do it?

As I thought about my teen's leaving, I also had to ask questions about myself: Am I ready for him to leave? How do I get myself ready so that this transition will be easier for him and for me? How do I prepare to let go?

So many challenges, so many questions, so many people with so many different answers.

Perhaps you have home schooled your kids and haven't had many problems, but now things are coming up that you didn't expect. Or you may have an only child, and with no others to compare her to, you wonder if she's normal. You may be a single parent, and you can't tell if you are overreacting or not taking something seriously enough.

We all second-guess our responses to our teens. And we often feel so responsible for the mistakes we see them making. There are no easy answers, no quick fixes, but there is reassurance in knowing other parents face the same challenges. Most of all, though, there is reassurance and comfort in remembering that our heavenly Father understands our teenagers, and He understand us and our challenges and joys as parents. He knows what is best for our kids—and what is best for us.

Focus Questions

Meditate on Psalm 34.

Get a new notebook or journal to use for your own study as you read this book. What you read will have far greater impact when you make your own notes. In the first section of your journal, write the following:

1. What are my fears as I parent teens (fears for myself, fears for my child)? Make a list of your fears. Be as specific as you can.

2. Look up the following passages and write down what each one says to you personally: Psalms 34:4, 17–18; 86:15–16; Romans 8:34; Hebrews 7:25.

3. Write out your own personal prayer to God. Tell Him your needs and desires for yourself and your teen. Ask Him to encourage you specifically as you read this book and as you share insights with other parents.

4. Leave several blank pages in your journal to record the specific ways that God answers your prayers during this study. As you read each chapter, write down practical things you learn that are helpful to you.

Meditate on Psalm 139. Insert your name and then your teen's name for each pronoun, making it your personal prayer.

> I sought the LORD, and he answered me;
>   he delivered me from all my fears.
>
> Psalm 34:4

2

Understanding This New Season

What's normal, what's not?

Struggling to contain my tears, I clenched my teeth in frustration. Externally I looked a mess; internally I felt like my heart was breaking. Mad, sad, angry, and fearful. I was in eighth grade, and I was miserable.

Even though it was past bedtime on a school night, I peeked into my parents' room to see if Mom was still up. Taking one look at my face, she laid aside her book and motioned to me to crawl onto the bed with her.

My tears began to flow freely as I curled up beside my mom.

"I'm so ugly!" I sobbed. "The cool girls don't want me to hang out with them. And the boys think I'm a dork. I don't like my teeth [buck teeth with heavily restraining braces], and I hate my glasses [very thick]. My hair looks stupid. And I'm bigger than all the boys! I'll never ever be popular or have the friends I want."

"Susan," my mom responded, "I know how you feel. I remember feeling the same way at your age. But I want you to know that your daddy and I think you are beautiful. You will have friends. Sometimes the girls who are the most popular in eighth grade fade out later on in high school. Your turn will come. Just hang on."

My wise mother didn't overreact. She knew that my emotional turmoil was normal. I did not need a panicky mom. I simply needed understanding and reassurance.

And I desperately needed hope.

I'm sure I didn't jump up and say, "Oh, Mother, you are so right!" More likely I left her bedside in tears, leaving her wondering if she'd handled me in the best way.

Yet forty years later I still remember that night. It was a night my mother gave me a tiny flicker of *hope*.

It's a New Season

Hopelessness grabs teenagers, but it also strikes parents of teens. Both of us lack hope in part because we lack perspective. Your teenage son doesn't make the varsity team as a freshman. He may automatically assume he'll never be the great player his best friend is. His hopes for acceptance are shattered; his life is "ruined." Feeling his son's disappointment, Dad wonders, *If only I'd practiced with my son more, then maybe... Am I partly to blame for my son's disappointment? Have I failed my son?*

What both father and son lack is perspective. Given some time and wisdom, this crisis won't seem nearly as crucial as it does at the moment. And much good can come out of it, even though *that* is not what either dad or son wants to hear right then.

Hopelessness is but one of the many emotions we are dealing with in this different season of parenting teens. We're into a new season with distinct challenges and, yes, unique blessings as well.

It helps to recognize that life is full of different seasons. There's the season of being newlyweds, the season of parenting toddlers, the season of parenting teens, the season of the empty nest, and the bungee cord season—when you think they've left, and they bounce back again! And there's the season of the golden years at the end of our lives. There are also mixed-up seasons like raising toddlers and teens at the same time, seasons of loss—when that spouse leaves or dies, when that grandchild doesn't come. There are seasons of joy and seasons of sorrow.

No season lasts forever.

Seeing life in terms of seasons will enable us to gain some perspective on the issues we face. Whatever season we are in, looking at the challenges and then choosing to focus on the blessings can give us comfort. We discover what's normal, what to expect, and what may lie ahead. We can stop wondering, *Am I the only one who . . . ?*

Just knowing what to expect will give us a head start in this new season of parenting teens. What's happening to them? What's happening to us? Are we normal? Are they? *Where* are the blessings?

What's Happening to Them?

Physically

Physically it seems an explosion has occurred. There are changes on every front. But the changes don't come in a way or on the timetable that our kids want. Either they develop too early or too late. For a girl, being the first to need a bra can be humiliating. But her best friend in seventh grade will be equally embarrassed as a late developer when a well-meaning adult says, "Now are *you* in fifth grade?"

Looks and wardrobe suddenly cause tears and frustration. Our daughter feels she is either too fat or too thin, too tall or too short. And there's the mushrooming problem of eating disorders—an ever-increasing challenge, especially for our girls.

Hormonal changes are hard on boys as well. You know your son is sensitive when he puts on a deep voice to answer the phone. If he's slight in build and his best friend is already developing muscle strength, he may feel "less than."

And he may be surprised at the amount of time he begins to spend thinking about girls. About sex. In our culture he is bombarded with visual images. And if he's on the Internet, he has easy access to pornography. A growing number of men and boys are struggling daily with this addiction. It's too available, too easy, and unfortunately not discussed as widely as it should be.

In their view of sex, our kids have moved from, "Yuck, I'd never want to do that!" to "If two people really love each other, is it realistic to expect them to wait until they are married?" And a growing number are being taught to question their own sexual identity. Some may wonder, "Could I be gay? What do I do with 'weird' feelings?" Troubling thoughts for a young teen.

Our teens always seem to be tired, and yet they have no trouble staying up until 2 A.M.! But then they have no trouble sleeping in until 2 P.M. when allowed. And if we want to know what's really happening in their lives, *we* have to stay up really late just in case they feel like talking.

It's a tiring, confusing time for our kids. Wise parents will remember what it was like when they were their age and then multiply that situation by at least ten. That will provide a better understanding of what our kids face in today's culture, with so many *more* voices dictating physical value.

Emotionally

"My son is twelve, and all of a sudden I'm stupid and boring," my friend LaVerne exclaimed. "Every year I emcee the student assembly at his school. After the assembly this year, he said to me, 'Mom, you really embarrassed me. You got up in front of everyone and you gave that stupid little wave and you said, "Hi, boys and girls," in that silly mother voice, "and you wore those stupid clogs and you didn't even have socks on . . .'"

"What has happened to my sweet, sensitive son?" LaVerne asked.

"You are an embarrassment right now. It's normal," I responded. "But don't worry, often by eleventh or twelfth grade you're no longer an embarrassment, and you begin to be acceptable again."

Embarrassment is but one of the several emotions that plague teens. And what causes their embarrassment will be determined to a large extent by their friends.

Mood swings, impacted by hormones and influenced by peers, will make them appear to be on a roller coaster. You never know if they will be up or down when they come in. They are likely to be hard to please. You will hear, "There's nothing to eat . . . nothing to wear . . . nothing to do." Adding to their frustration is the fact that they can't explain why they feel the way they do and why they are so hard to please.

The emotional roller coaster can be particularly hard on sibling relationships. You may have thought you'd experienced a thaw in sibling rivalry during those middle years, and you were actually seeing some sibling friendships begin to develop. But now the short fuses seem to be undermining the small steps of progress that had been made.

Often there is other emotional tension in the home. You may be struggling through a marital separation or caring for an aging parent or losing a job. These extra stresses will also impact your teen.

As our kids walk through this season of emotional turmoil, they need hope. A daughter needs to hear us say, "Sweetie, I want you to know that I understand this is a hard time in your life—sometimes you feel great about yourself, other times you don't like yourself, and occasionally you don't especially like us. It's all normal, and we will come through this time. You are a special girl, and I love you. We will get through this season."

Often simply saying out loud what's going on inside communicates understanding and alleviates some of the tension.

Socially

One word captures this season socially: *awkward.* Our kids are trying on different personality types to see what fits best. One day your son may be "Mr. Cool," the next a clown or a tough guy. Your daughter may be the friendliest or the silliest, the most talkative or the most private. It's exhausting for the family who's also trying to figure out who this kid is. It's equally frustrating to the teen who isn't sure who he *wants* to be. At this age, who he wants to be will be determined to a large extent by his friends. What friends think may become more important for the moment than family values. Right now, identity and acceptance are based upon friends' opinions, not upon a parent's wishes.

Complicating this picture is the fact that friends change. Your daughter's "absolute-best-friend-forever" may suddenly have become "persona non grata." And those girls your daughter wouldn't have anything to do with last year because they were "so snobby" may now be her best friends.

Girls can be brutal to each other. Rare is the teenage girl who makes it through a year without being "mortally" wounded by another or being hurtful herself. These painful times can become valuable learning opportunities in how to care for others. Being hurt ourselves can make us more sensitive, more careful not to be the one who excludes. But it takes a wise parent to draw out the parallels for the teen.

As a parent of both boys and girls, I believe these social challenges are more volatile with the girls. Generally, boys don't seem to hurt each other as much, and they appear to be less sensitive. Yet they too have tender hearts, and they too need friends. Some kids are happy with one friend. Others seem to need a group. Each child will have different relationship needs, and your child's needs may be different from yours. That's okay.

Mentally

We've moved from the fun of the ABCs to the pressures of the SATs. And often our teens feel they're in a no-win situation. Either they are bored and not challenged enough, or they are in over their heads and seriously wonder if they can make it. It's easy for them to feel like they can't satisfy us. We always want more. When they look at all that's on their plate for the coming week, they slide into an immobile depression because "there's just no way . . ." Perhaps there is a learning disability, an inability to concentrate, an overcommitment to extracurricular activities, too much time on a job, or a lack of self-discipline. Or perhaps they feel their parents are too busy with their own issues to really care how they are doing academically. It's easy for them to feel frustrated. Add to this the pressure for the right college, the must-have scholarship, the competition for the right job, and our teen wilts in frustration.

Friends play a part in mental pressures. If friends think academics are important, your child will too. If being smart is uncool, a gifted child might hide his abilities. Usually by the junior or senior year, your teen will begin to perform more according to his own abilities than to conform to social pressure. But you can't wait until then to raise the GPA. The ninth-grade year begins the averages. These will play a big part in determining college choices, so the pressure is great even for the young teen.

Spiritually

Ray has been in a private Christian school since kindergarten. His parents, both strong leaders in evangelical circles, have always made their kids a priority. Yet at seventeen Ray is struggling with his faith. Recently he said to his mom, "I'm not sure I buy all this Christian stuff anymore. I can show you lots of intellectuals who don't believe."

This is a season of weaning. Of questioning. Of doubting. But it can lead to a season of owning. It's not unusual for a teen to wonder, *Why do I believe what I've been taught? Do I really want to believe? What about . . . ?*

During this season a necessary shift is beginning to take place. Our teens must begin to shift from a dependence upon our faith to their own more personal dependence upon God. And this shift will likely involve some questioning. It may be hard for the teen who assumes he's being disloyal or who feels shame for questioning. It can also be an intentional ploy of a rebellious teen to *get at* his parents. Our kids have to know that there is nothing wrong with questioning. We must give them room to question, but we must challenge them to pursue the answers as well.

Often we as parents make one of two mistakes. Either we criticize our teens for questioning and provide them with simplistic, legalistic answers, or we applaud their questioning without encouraging them to seek answers and without taking the time to point them to good resources that will help them.

It has been said that God has no grandchildren. He only has children. Each of us must come to the place where ours is a *personal* faith, not an *inherited* faith. It will comfort our teens to know that their questioning doesn't shake us and it doesn't shake God. We have faith that God has His hand firmly on them.

What's Happening to Us?

Emotionally

When my kids got through those exhausting toddler years, I thought that things were beginning to calm down. I even thought those middle years were fun. They still wanted to cuddle, to hold hands in public, to ask my advice. They sometimes even offered to help with the dishes without being asked. And it was just plain fun to be together. I seemed to know what would make them happy, and they were unabashed in their childhood enthusiasm.

In a way I pictured our family like a giant jigsaw puzzle. After an overwhelming start on those two thousand puzzle pieces, I had finally managed to put the border together. And I had a pile of green puzzle pieces that looked like they would fit together to complete one section of the puzzle. My puzzle seemed to be falling nicely into place. And *then* I had teenagers. And I felt like someone had picked up my carefully laid out puzzle and dumped it out all over the floor again.

My identity as a parent was in question again. My self-image was shaky. My emotions were tender.

The season of parenting teens is an emotional one for parents. It's especially challenging for a single parent. You don't have anyone to balance you, to say, "Honey, you're taking this too seriously," or "It isn't as bad as it seems," or "This *is* serious."

Not only do we question what we're doing, but our teens also see our weaknesses more clearly. They point out our inconsistencies. We feel inadequate.

Our teens don't need us as much, either. As they begin to pull away, we sense a loss, a pain, one that we know is only going to grow.

With toddlers we were physically exhausted; now we're emotionally exhausted. Our kids' arguments are far more sophisticated. All of a sudden we feel stupid. What is right? Who is right?

Socially

We too are struggling with peer pressure. It centers around *the other parent*. Her kids have high SATs; her son is the star athlete, the class leader, the one who's polite to adults, who wears nice clothes to church. And mine . . . well. Where did I go wrong?

Looking at another parent and comparing ourselves is a big mistake. We will either become critical of that other parent, or we will become down on ourselves. We must learn from one another and be encouraged by each other, but we must not fall into the trap of comparing ourselves, our mate, or our child to another. We are a unique family. Each of our children is special, with different levels of ability, different callings in life.

Our calendar can be challenging during this season. There are so many demands on our time. We feel pressure from our friends, our families, and our colleagues. It can become easy to find family members passing each other in the night on the way to the next car pool, the next meeting. How do we decide what is right for us?

Physically

A friend recently called to say, "I've discovered God's big mistake! Why did He make many of our kids hit the teen years at the same time we hit menopause?"

If this is true for you, you do have a house full of hormones. And you and especially Dad will need a sense of humor. Or perhaps, like my friend Holly, you find yourself expecting a new baby while at the same time parenting teens! Hormones are wacky. But it's nice to be able to blame things on hormones.

Depending on your family situation, this can be a physically exhausting season. Perhaps you have lost a parent, or your spouse has left. It has been a season of grief. When my dad died unexpectedly, we all went through a difficult time. But what we weren't prepared for was the physical exhaustion. Grief is work. It's emotional exhaustion, and it leads to physical exhaustion. If you are experiencing grief of any sort during this season, you are tired. It's normal. Just knowing why helps alleviate some of the tension.

Mentally

Our high school degree, our college degree, even our graduate degree isn't much help in rearing kids. And all those experts seem to disagree, even the Christian ones. There is just too much information. Too many "right" formulas.

Perhaps you feel well equipped at programming computers, solving a complex engineering problem, prosecuting a case, or cashing in on the market, but when it comes to raising teens you seem to be inept. You don't seem to do anything right. You seem to score a big, fat zero.

All of a sudden we are "mentally challenged." Three of our kids need to use two cars at the same time. And they have to know *right now* how we are going to solve this. We have to get children to five different activities in the next couple of hours and also get everyone fed. We weren't taught how to do this in our math classes.

Raising teens can be especially hard for the Type A personality, the natural problem solver. Those of us who are natural problem solvers look at a problem and offer three quick ways to solve it. But it's not always that easy to "fix" a teen.

Spiritually

We may find ourselves wondering, *God, do You really care, do You really hear?*

We may feel presumptuous praying about something as seemingly inconsequential as a prom date for an awkward daughter, a friend for a lonely seventh grader. After all, some people are dying; some have no food to eat. Why should I bother God with this?

We may feel guilty because we don't seem to have time to nurture our own relationship with God. Things are so busy right now. And we're ashamed because we know we've let God down in so many ways ourselves. Who are we to expect Him to bless our kids?

But He does hear. He does care. In fact, He delights in us—and in our kids. And yes, He knows all those ways we've failed Him.

But He still cares. He still has the power to redeem. He still longs to work in our lives and in the lives of our children. He still pours out His love. As parents and as teens, our common need is hope. He is our Hope. Nothing is too difficult for Him.

Hope is restored when we honestly articulate the challenges but then choose to focus on our blessings. And when we remember that God is faithful.

A Season of Blessing?

Yes, the teen years can be a season of tremendous blessing.

During these years we begin to see the payoff of that early training—we begin to relate to them more as adults. They can be fun to talk with. We can ask their advice. We can do things together that we both enjoy. We begin to see their unique gifts more clearly and to understand how God has uniquely packaged them. We watch with pride as they learn how to relate to our adult friends. They did learn some manners after all! As they come through the teen years, they seem to be more confident in who they are. They are not as embarrassed by being with us.

We notice signs of thoughtfulness and glimpses of wisdom. With time, we have gained a little perspective, and we realize those things we feared were so crucial weren't as important as we thought. We have had more chances to experience God's faithfulness, especially in the desperate times with our children. Looking back we see He *was* there. He *was* at work even though we couldn't see it at that time. Because we've prayed over the years, we have a savings account of answered prayers. This will enable us to trust Him more in the future.

In all honesty, I must confess that the teen years for me have been my favorite season. No, they have not been without difficult challenges. Yes, there have been times of despair. But on the whole I have enjoyed this season more than any other. We are each uniquely different and we will each like different seasons. But be encouraged. Your children's teen years can be the best of your life! It is important in the midst of the difficulties to look for the blessings. It's all too easy to focus on the problems and overlook the good things that are happening. If we take time to thank God for the specific blessings, He will lift our anxiety and concern and restore our perspective.

As we struggle with ourselves in this season, it's helpful to realize that God has handpicked each of our families. He has given us the exact children we need in the exact birth order with their unique personalities. He has chosen each child to be His tool in our lives to mold us into the men and women He created us to be. He's given us that strong-willed child, that child with ADD, that child who clashes with us, that difficult stepchild, that one who has run away, and yes, even that stillborn child. Each child is a precious gift from Him. And He will use each child in our lives for good as we let Him.

Our hope is renewed when we remember that these are first of all *His kids*—and so are we.

He loves each of our children more than we do, and He knows them much better than we do.

He also loves *us*—their imperfect, ill-equipped parents—and He has chosen *us* to raise these little ones. But He has not left us to do it alone. He has promised to be there.

Focus Questions

Meditate on Psalm 16.

1. How does God encourage King David in this psalm? How does this song encourage you specifically in this season of parenting teenagers?
2. What has been a difficult challenge for you during this season of parenting teens?
3. Is God using a particular child in your life? What is He teaching you through this child?
4. What are some blessings for you personally during this season?

Meditate on Ephesians 1:15–23. Make this your personal prayer for the coming week.

> I have set the LORD always before me.
> Because he is at my right hand,
>   I will not be shaken.
>
> Psalm 16:8

3

Creating an Atmosphere of Encouragement

Walking on eggshells?

As a teenager I remember going to a sleepover at Kate's house. She was part of the "cool" crowd, so I felt honored being invited to her house. Yet at the same time I felt uncomfortable.

Standing on the front steps of her huge home, I rang the bell. Her mother answered the door and, barely looking at me, remarked in a sullen voice, "Oh, it's you. Kate's in her room." Turning away, she yelled, "Kate, your friend is here, but your room *better* be clean before you come out."

Without another word Kate's mom walked away.

Kate and I were left to ourselves for most of the evening. There didn't seem to be any planned dinner, so we just fixed our own. Kate's younger brothers got into a fight over a new soccer ball and began to scream and kick each other. When their dad finally came home, he threw his briefcase on the floor, and looking past Kate and me, lashed out at his sons, "Why did you boys leave the bikes in the drive? Get out there right this minute and put them away!"

Kate's mom ignored him and continued working at her desk. Throughout the evening there was little conversation between family members. The boys stayed glued to the TV, and Kate and I listened to her latest music. At bedtime I couldn't fall asleep because I could hear her parents yelling at one another in the other room. Kate didn't seem the least bit uncomfortable or embarrassed. Apparently, this was normal family life for her. I, on the other hand, was relieved when morning finally came and I went home.

Mary Ellen's home was different from Kate's in every way. It was a tiny duplex, and Mary Ellen's mom was a single parent. Because she lived next door to me, I often ran over for a quick visit.

Opening the front door, Mary Ellen's mom would exclaim, "Oh, Susan, I'm so glad to see you; do come in. How about something to eat?" As we sat around the kitchen table, she'd ask, "How was school today? Did that boy you have a crush on talk to you in the hall? How'd you do on that awful algebra test?"

As Mary Ellen and I visited with her mom, she would tell us hilarious stories about some of her students. A college professor, she encouraged us to study. Often our conversation would end with a lighthearted yet serious, "This is fun, but it's time to hit the homework, girls." And we knew she meant it. With a hug good-bye I'd head next door to my homework, encouraged and challenged but with a sense of well-being.

Two different homes, two different atmospheres. One marked by sullenness, angry words, disinterest, and tension.

The other marked by an interest in each other, laughter, acceptance, and warmth. I doubt Kate's parents were aware of the negative atmosphere in their home. They loved their kids. They had not intentionally set out to create a home with the tension theirs possessed. They had just succumbed to it.

Sometimes my home succumbs to a musty, dank smell. Often I don't even realize the house smells bad until one of the kids walks in the front door and says, "Mom, it stinks in here. You better put on the 'smells pot!'" And so out comes a kitchen pot in which I mix whole cloves, whole allspice, whole cinnamon, and a little water to simmer. It doesn't take long for this sweet aroma to pervade the house.

In a similar way, it's easy for us to let the atmosphere of our home slip into a place of tension, hostility, or emotional disconnectedness. Our home can become merely a way station in which the family members stop in to eat and sleep on their way to their next event.

In a house with teenagers there will inevitably be times of tension. It's *a given* with this season. Yet day in and day out we want the atmosphere in our home to be one of encouragement. But encouraging, positive atmospheres don't just happen. They are intentionally created.

Why is the atmosphere in our home so important?

The atmosphere in the home will determine the type of communication we build with our teen. It will determine how we deal with hot topics, how we set limits and let go. If the atmosphere is already one of friction, how can we hope to have a sensible conversation about the party *she* wants to attend? If there is disrespect already, how can we possibly avoid the shouting match when *he* isn't given permission to take the car? If there is already an emotional disconnectedness, why would our child *want* to share his fears with us? If there is a continual feeling of walking on eggshells in our home, how will we react to one another in the normal crises that our teens will encounter?

It's helpful to recognize two tendencies. The *first* is our tendency to focus all our attention on how we should handle the hot topics with our kids—drinking, sex, drugs, eating disorders, pornography, and others. To look for the quick fix, for the right counselor. After all, we're desperate, we're busy, and we need the bottom line. But how we handle these hard issues will be directly determined by the relationship we have cultivated with our child. That relationship is a reflection of the atmosphere in our home.

We need to create a positive atmosphere in our home because that enables us to build strong relationships with our teens. These relationships will make it possible to work through the tough issues together rather than allowing the hard times to pull us apart.

The *second* tendency is to think it's already too late. A tearful friend called me this morning. "We had another confrontation with our son last night," she said. "I don't think I handled it right. I feel like nothing I do is right. I pray, but I still feel so inadequate. Every decision I make seems wrong. He is miserable. We are miserable. There is nothing I do that makes him happy. The tension in our home is depressing. I feel like we've blown it, and it's too late to change anything—and I wouldn't know how to change anyway."

From God's perspective it's never too late. He can always redeem. He knows us, and He knows our child. He is at work even if we can't see it at the moment. But it is also never too late to make changes in the atmosphere in our homes. It may be one small change that enables a tightly wound person to become open, one tiny step that will spark a glimmer of hope.

When my kids said that my house smelled bad, I had to take specific steps to change the atmosphere. I intentionally chose three ingredients for my "smells pot" that I knew would help make a positive difference. And then I waited for the results to slowly permeate the house.

It took longer for my pleasant aroma to reach some areas of the house than others. And the change was gradual. But ultimately the spicy cinnamon smell evoked a response: "Wow, Mom, it sure smells cozy in here!"

If we want to create an atmosphere of encouragement, we must be intentional. We will either succumb to a negative atmosphere or be proactive in creating a positive one.

Being intentional will involve assessment. Take a look at the home in which you grew up. What was the atmosphere like? What made you feel comfortable, secure, accepted? What made you want to come home? On the other hand, was there anything you disliked? Was there anything that made coming home unpleasant? What seemed to cause tension or distance? What would you like to emulate from your childhood home, and what would you like to change?

Consider the following seven ingredients as you contemplate what you want your home to feel like.

Security

A strong-willed first child in her family, Sally is always pushing the limits. When her parents are firm, she responds, "You are the meanest parents in town!" and storms to her room. When they attempt to be flexible, it's never good enough for her.

The bottom line is that even though she's unaware of it, Sally wants to call the shots in the family. Fears of damaging their daughter's self-image and of alienating themselves from her have made her parents hesitant in saying no.

More than anything, they want Sally to feel secure in their love. But security is not built when a child realizes that she calls the shots. God does not intend for a child to have that much power over her parents. Security is built when a child knows that her parents call the shots. They love her, will listen to her, will grow in releasing her, but she is not the boss. She is the child. They are the parents. She can count on them to mean what they say. She instinctively knows there's a line she must not cross, and thus she respects them. This gives her a sense of security.

One of the hardest things in parenting teenagers is discerning when to stand firm and when to flex. We will look at this in more detail in chapter 5, but before we handle the particulars, it is crucial to establish an atmosphere in which it is clear that the parent is in charge. Being in charge does not mean being a dictator. It means exerting loving leadership in the nurturing of our children. This type of leadership instills a sense of security in our child.

Security is increased when the child knows what matters to the parents. Is it money, success, the right friends, the best grades? Or is it character—integrity, compassion, respect, generosity, faith?

Several years ago we asked ourselves this question. We came to believe that it is character that will sustain a child, an adult, a family. This question led Johnny and me to write *Character Matters! Raising Kids with Values That Last*.[1] As parents we want to raise confident children with a sense of destiny—kids who know who they are and where they are going. We want these things for ourselves as well. But character isn't something we get and then just pass on to our children. All of our lives we too are growing; we never finish. The character traits that each of us values will be evident in the atmosphere of our home. If I value integrity, I will not joke at the dinner table about getting away with not paying that parking ticket or fudging on my income taxes. Instead, I will pay the ticket or the taxes and share with my kids that even though I really wanted to "get away with it," I've learned that personal integrity is far more important.

Like it or not, our child will look to us as role models. We can be a mom or a dad she will one day (not now—but in the distant future!) want to emulate, or we can be one whose imprint she will spend much of her life trying to erase. Our kids aren't looking for perfect parents. They know more than anyone that there aren't any. What they need isn't perfect parents but honest ones who are trying to live a consistent life of growing in character themselves.

A secure home will be one in which there is both verbal and physical affection. I remember my dad saying to me, "Susan, I love you so much."

"Why, Daddy?" I would respond.

"Just because you're mine," he'd reply.

It wasn't because I'd made the honor roll or won the ball game or been kind to my siblings. I hadn't done any of these things. It was just because I belonged to him.

His unconditional love gave me a sense of security.

Perhaps you never heard those words from your parents. You may still carry wounds from your past. There is good news. *You* can be the first of a generation of healthy families.

Even if it's awkward, say it. Even if it's hard for you to be an affectionate parent, hug your kids. Even when that teen doesn't respond, do it anyway. Most teens will go through a period when they don't want hugs, especially in public. But do it in private anyway. Even if they are cold as a fish. Don't expect a response now. Your job is to keep doing it. One day they will eventually warm up.

Sometimes when we look at our kids we wonder if God didn't make a mistake. Our personalities totally clash. We don't understand one another. There's one with whom we can't get to first base. One we love but just don't especially like. We feel shame and guilt. After all, we're the parent, and we don't know what to do. We feel insecure. We know God has given us these children to raise, to influence, to train up, but it's so hard, so painful. When we hit these rough spots, we have to remember that God chose our exact kids so that through them we would come to understand in a deeper way His love for us—His "often difficult teens." When we rest in this assurance, we will be more likely to communicate a sense of security to our teens that says, "You are accepted, you are wanted, you are valued in this home."

Time

Spending time with someone communicates that he or she is valuable. We know this; we believe it. Why, then, is it so hard to do? In today's world we are overwhelmed with options, too many options on how to spend our money, our time, too many activities to choose from. It wouldn't be so difficult if many of the choices weren't so good. Often it isn't an issue between bad and good but between good and good. There are options for Dad, for Mom, for each child, for the whole family—options that compete. And there's peer pressure for both teens and parents. We fall prey to it as well. This happened to me.

I was at a basketball game in which our twins were playing. As I sat with two other moms we began to chat, actually to impress each other with how stressed we were!

"I hope this game ends soon," one mother said sighing. "My daughter has a select team she's also playing on, and we have to rush over to that practice. Then tomorrow I have to go to her music ensemble recital, and an hour after that she has a field trip with this accelerated class she's taking."

"Oh, I know what you mean," the other mom responded. "My daughter has the lead in the school play and rehearsal starts in an hour! She's also in the advanced ballet class, which has a performance next week. And then there's this great extra-credit opportunity for her Spanish class . . ."

Listening to my two friends, I began to feel "less than." My daughters weren't involved in so many activities. *Oh my, I moaned to myself, if I were a better mom I'd take advantage of these options.* Walking slowly out of the gym, I decided I'd better go home and sign my girls up for some more extracurricular activities!

I had fallen prey to a parental peer pressure—the pressure that says whoever has the most involved child is the best parent.

We need to stop and ask ourselves the question, In ten years what will matter the most? Will it matter most that our child won yet another trophy or that we said no to one more team and instead sat down to family dinner together? In the long run, do we want to collect trophies that will only gather dust on a closet shelf, or do we want to invest in building family friendships that will last a lifetime?

Hard questions with no easy answers.

Each of us will have to determine what is right for us in our particular season of life. Each of us will have to say no, and we will not be popular for it. Our teens are likely to pitch a fit. They will not understand the need for family time. Don't expect them to. It's unrealistic. Part of our responsibility as parents is to take the long-range view. Our long-range view holds that it is important to build relationships between siblings, and that building relationships involves spending time together.

Not only do we need to have scheduled time together as a family, but we also need simply to be available to our teens. Much has been made about the issue of quantity versus quality time. It's not an either/or—it's a both/and. You cannot program a teenager for quality time. You have to hang around just in case they are struck with the urge to have a personal conversation with you. It will most likely be at an inconvenient time—late at night or when you're right in the middle of a project. But we have to stop and seize this rare opportunity.

We may go to great lengths to spend some time with our teen. We may have to cancel a meeting, give up a golf game, decline an invitation. And then our time with them turns out not to be a special bonding time but an awkward time of silence or an unpleasant confrontation. And we wonder, *Why do I even try?* It's easy to give up because we feel like such a failure as a parent. It's easier to run back to the office. *There* we are appreciated at least a little bit, and there we feel like we make some progress. At the office we have some measure of success, but at home we feel like a failure.

Part of our problem is that we are looking for instant results. Instead of expecting the investment of time with our teen to produce a quick dividend, we need to view these times as a long-term investment that will one day reap the dividend of a healthy relationship with our child.

Openness

Something was bothering Alex. His mom could tell that her middle son, a high school freshman, just wasn't himself. It wasn't any one thing; he just seemed sad and disconnected. After observing her son and praying about what to do, she sat on his bed one evening, and as she scratched his back she said, "Son, something's going on with you. I'd like it if you would tell me about it."

"Oh, Mom," he began, and burst into tears. "I'm just really lonely. I thought going to this new school would be so much easier than it is. I don't ever get to see my older brother. He already has friends here, and even though my friend Ben is here, he doesn't have time for me either. Since he came last year, he already has new friends he'd rather be with than me."

As his mom listened, he continued to pour out his wounded heart. She didn't have any answers for him. He didn't really want any. He just needed Mom to listen, to empathize, and to comfort. Before leaving, she put her arms around this lanky son and prayed for him. Sharing in his pain and taking it to God together drew mother and son closer.

Creating an atmosphere that encourages openness in a home is crucial. We want our kids to feel safe in sharing their hurts and questions with us. We want there to be a freedom from fear in our homes.

I remember my dad saying, "Susan, I want you to know that I will not always agree with what you say or do, but I'll always be here for you."

Both Mom and Dad were firm disciplinarians, and although I didn't like it at the time, I did respect them. I always knew that no matter what I'd done, I could tell them, and they would help me.

Our kids will feel safe in coming to us when they know we will take them seriously, when they know we won't laugh at them, when they know we will take the time to listen and not make snap judgments, and when they know we are committed to them no matter what.

We may have one child who tells us everything. In fact, we wish she wouldn't tell us so much. And her brother may be closed up tighter than a drum. We'd faint if he ever shared anything personal.

We can encourage a spirit of openness as we share personally with our teens. We can share a failure or disappointment that we have experienced, or share an area that we want to grow in and ask them to pray for us. Recently I shared with my son a bad attitude I had toward a friend. It stemmed from some hurt she had caused me, but I knew I had to let it go, and I was having a hard time doing so. Talking about it with my son and asking him to pray for me encouraged me to put the issue behind me and move forward rather than letting bitterness creep in.

Certainly we don't want to burden our kids, and we must be wise in what we share. But as they join us in the adult years, it reassures them to know that we too struggle, and we too need their prayers.

Respect

"You b——," seventeen-year-old Elsie screamed at her mother as she slammed the door. Her weary mother just stood there in silence. It was an all-too-familiar scene.

A positive atmosphere and flagrant, verbal disrespect do not mix. We must not allow verbal abuse of parents or of siblings. Most kids talk back, and if it is not dealt with when they are very small, it will increase in the teen years.

So what do we do? We do not permit it—ever. We have stiff consequences for back talk, and we follow through.

As a parent, we have to honestly ask ourselves the question, *How is my speech?* Sometimes a teen is only mimicking what they have grown up hearing their parents do. We may need help and accountability to clean up our own language. It's a wise, humble dad who goes to his son and says, "Your rudeness to your mother is no longer acceptable. I realize that I have a problem with verbal abuse. I too am rude to your mom and to you and your sisters. I want you to pray for me and to call me on it when you hear me speak in an unkind way. Both of us need to change our ways."

It may also be crucial for you, the parent, to get counseling or to be held accountable by another adult. How we talk to each other is too important to treat lightly. You are training future husbands and wives in how to treat their mates. Do you want your daughter spoken to by her husband in the manner in which you are speaking to your wife?

What if your mate doesn't think he or she has a problem? It is still your responsibility not to permit your child to verbally abuse you. It will be hard, but do it anyway. If you do not stop the abuse, your child will grow to dislike you because she cannot respect you. You let her get away with something she should not have been permitted to get away with. If you are a single parent, ask another couple to walk through this change with you. They may need to sit with you and your child and discuss this together.

While our words signify our respect of each other as people, we must also respect another's possessions. Teach your kids that they must ask before they borrow anything. The item must be returned promptly, neat and clean. In a house with girls who wear each other's clothes, this is especially important. Borrowed cars must be filled with gas and returned clean. "Always leave something in better shape than you found it" is an ageless axiom that underlines consideration. It's thoughtfulness. It's respect.

One of the ways that we can show our teens we respect them is by asking their opinions. They often have insights we don't, and we need their input. They are better at some things than we are, and we need their help. My girls have a better sense of fashion than I do. Consequently, I don't go shopping without them. They dress me. I ask them what I should wear when I go to their events. I don't want to embarrass them! Last weekend at a football game, one of their friends said, "Mrs. Yates, you look so sharp. How do you do it?"

"It's the girls," I replied. "They are my personal shoppers!"

Appreciation

Trying to maintain a 3.8 GPA, playing a varsity sport, serving as class president, and leading worship in his youth group was causing Ben, a junior, to become irritable and frustrated. His relationship with his parents was usually good, but lately he had no time for them or for his siblings. He was simply running on overload. And he was exhausted.

Neurologist Phillip Pearl of the Children's National Medical Center in Washington, D.C., says, "The average American teen is chronically fatigued. And it's gotten worse over the years, not better."[2] With this sleep issue in mind, two large school systems in northern Virginia have been studying the possibility of a split shift that would allow some high schools to start later in the day to make it possible for teens to get more sleep.

More and more teens are finding it hard to fit homework in around emailing and visiting chat rooms on the Internet. And with competition growing for admittance to good colleges, the importance of resumé building begins earlier and earlier. The guidance counselor says try for one school, Mom and Dad insist on another, while friends have a different slant on what's best. So many people with expectations!

All of this adds up to one thing for our kids: stress.

Our tendency as parents will be to fuss at our teens for how they are managing their time. But before we hit them with a new time management plan, we need to appreciate the stress they are under.

It is not always wise to fix a situation. Sometimes it's best merely to offer compassion and understanding.

"Son, I just want you to know that I appreciate all the stress you must be feeling with your schedule, and with everyone giving you advice. You are working so hard, and I know you are exhausted. I'm proud of you, and I'm praying for you."

Bake some cookies and put them on his pillow with a note. Write him a note of encouragement and put it in his backpack. Send him an email from your office with a word of appreciation saying that you understand his stress.

Letting our teens know we appreciate the stress they are under makes a huge difference. It also helps to tell them we appreciate their growth toward maturity and responsibility.

Intentionally look for small steps of growth and point them out to your child. He *did* work on a paper two days before it was due instead of leaving it until the night before. Compliment him. He *did* say no to something he really wanted to do because of an already full plate. Praise him. He *did* remember to put gas in the car. Thank him.

It's all too easy for us to fall into the trap of *encore parenting*. Parenting that says, "This is good, but I know you can do better next time." He gets a 90 percent on a quiz, and you push for a 95 next time. She makes a goal in the soccer game, and you have a strategy that will enable her to score more in the next game. For those of us who are driven, it will be extremely hard simply to rejoice in the accomplishment at hand without wanting an encore. But encore parents are never satisfied. There's always something more that can be done. Perhaps you grew up in a home where you never quite did enough. As hard as you tried, it was never quite good enough. And today you still feel you don't quite measure up. No matter what you do, you can't please "them." We do not want to be encore parents. Yes, we want our kids to excel, but there is a time simply to appreciate what has been done without looking ahead to the next accomplishment.

Appreciate their developing character growth as more important than their accomplishments. Children come into the world packaged differently. One has the capacity for a 4.0 GPA. Another will be doing his best simply to graduate from high school. One has been given the gift of music. Another seems to have no upfront gifts that others will notice, yet he has a compassionate heart. One has an IQ of 150, while his sibling has Down's syndrome. We can praise that A or that stellar musical performance, but we must take care that the bulk of our praise is for character development. It is character development that matters the most. A Down's syndrome daughter needs a celebration as she learns to feed herself. "Honey, you are trying so hard! I am so proud of the way you worked until you got it!" Explain to her siblings that she has shown amazing persistence.

To the quiet child who stops to help the neighbor carry in her groceries, comment, "I'm so proud of the way you are growing in thoughtfulness. It's a wonderful trait."

To the daughter who spends most of the season on the bench cheering for her teammates who get to play, say, "I know you are disappointed not to play, but I see that you are growing in endurance and in encouragement as you cheer for your teammates. Your character and your mature attitude make me more proud of you than if you were first-string!"

Wisdom

One of the rich blessings in this season of parenting teens is that you can begin to explain some things to them and they will begin to "get it." Wisdom is coming!

Your fourteen-year-old daughter bursts through the front door—again in tears.

"I had to sit by myself at lunch today. Ellen and Amy [the 'cool' girls] didn't save me a seat, and I had nowhere to sit. I don't think they like me anymore. And my art teacher didn't act like he liked my project. What if he thinks I'm terrible? And those jocks were making fun of my friend Terry, who's really short. I felt so embarrassed for him. And . . ."

As the tears and the words tumble out, you sit there exhausted by the pain and agony in this sensitive child. She's always been the one most easily hurt. The one you only have to look at in the wrong way and she dissolves into tears, the one who grieves over a wounded animal, the one most hurt by her peers.

How can you help this tender child of yours?

It's time to explain gifts and weaknesses.

"Sweetie, I want to talk to you about gifts and weaknesses. Each of us has been carefully and uniquely designed by God. Each of us has special gifts. God has made you very sensitive. You care deeply about people, and you hurt for them. Your sensitivity is a gift. God will use this gift of yours in amazing ways as you grow up. There was a great woman named Mother Teresa who had this same gift. Her sensitivity grew into compassion, and she was used by God to impact the lives of many people all over the world. God may one day use you in similar ways. But Sweetie, every gift has a flat side or a weakness. The flat side of your gift is that you are easily hurt. You can overreact or assume the worst in how someone views you. You will have to toughen up and guard against overreacting. You will be working on this for the rest of your life. One of the positive ways that you can use this gift right now is to care for those in your class who are lonely. Part of your gift is being able to sense someone's pain. Do you know anyone who is new in your class, or someone who's going through a hard time in their family? Perhaps you could ask them to sit with you at lunch. You can be an encouragement to them. I am so thankful that God has made you in this way!"

It's helpful to share with your child one of your own gifts and its accompanying weaknesses and how you are trying to grow in balancing the weaknesses. Ask her to pray for you.

If appropriate, clue in her teacher. Let her know that your child is especially sensitive and that you are working to use this in positive ways. Suggest that if she knows of a lonely, new student in class, she might consider asking your daughter to be the newcomer's guide for the day. Anything the teacher can do to build up the positive side of this gift will be an encouragement.

Ask God to reveal to you the gifts and weaknesses of your child. They are more apparent now that your child is older. Talk with your child about how you see her. Stress the positive. Point her to a role model with similar gifts. This gives her a vision. Share your own weaknesses. Your openness will make her feel more like an adult, and it will give her some perspective. Give her a suggestion for using her gift in a positive way starting now. Wisdom comes with age and experience. We will grow in wisdom along with our teens as we walk through these uncharted years together.

Celebration

It was the middle school costume party and dance, and I was determined to play a joke on our son John, an eighth grader. Since he was one of the oldest students and hence felt more secure, I figured I could get away with it. So I dressed up in a large man's raincoat, tucked my hair under my bald-man's cap, put on my funky plastic nose, weird glasses, and mustache, and went to the dance! A couple of the girls in his school knew what I was up to and began to laugh and whisper as I asked my son to dance. The room was dark and full of dancing teens. He had no clue who I was and didn't quite know how to respond, so away we danced. Finally, as the laughter and giggles spread, I too burst out laughing, and he said, "Oh, no—Mom, it's not you!"

Humbly put, I was the talk of the evening! Now, I wouldn't have done that to my daughter. She would have been humiliated. And I wouldn't have done it to John a year earlier. But in this situation it worked! And it set a precedent. Recently this same son flew home from a semester in England. All the family gathered in anticipation at the airport to welcome him home. When the last person had come off the plane, we became concerned. Where was he? Looking for my blonde son, I didn't notice the weird soul in tacky silky pajamas, oversized grotesque shades, and huge, black curly hair walking out into the crowded lobby pushing his luggage toward me. Everyone began to snicker and laugh. You can imagine my astonishment and his thrill when he came face-to-face with me and said, "Hi, Mom, I gottcha!"

Some of the members of our family (mostly the males!) have an addiction to ice cream. Every now and then at the oddest moments, my husband announces that he hears the old car groaning. It just has to go. It needs it. Studying comes to a halt, chores are put aside, and we all pile in the car and head to the local Ben and Jerry's to get some ice cream. Silly perhaps. Simple yes. But oh, how we need to celebrate as families.

We need to laugh and be crazy together. One of my regrets is that we haven't laughed enough. We haven't done enough crazy things. We've taken life far too seriously. A house full of parents and teens especially needs laughter. Let me encourage you to do something simply for fun this week. Not something that's expensive, time consuming, or that's a big deal. But something totally out of character, just for fun.

We want the atmosphere in our homes to reflect joy. We want our home to be a secure, safe, and fun place to go. Often we have to work at the fun component. But it's well worth it.

I've been boiling chicken. My house smells, and it isn't pleasant. I need to open the windows for a few minutes to air out the unpleasant aroma and then put the "smells pot" on to begin to change the aroma throughout my home. I know I'll have to do it again in the future. I'll always have to be adjusting the aroma. Sometimes I won't notice it's bad until a family member tells me. Occasionally I'll try a fresh potpourri instead of my smells pot. Often I make a poor choice; it's too sweet or thick or antiseptic. Other times I find a winner.

The atmosphere in our homes may have become toxic. Sometimes someone else will have to point out a problem for us. We may make poor choices as we seek to bring about change. It will take longer to get rid of some tension than we wish. But it's never too late to change. And we have the Spirit of a loving Father to guide us as we take positive steps.

Focus Questions

Meditate on Colossians 3.

1. Consider the home in which you were raised. What would you like to carry over into the atmosphere of

your own home? Is there anything you'd like to leave out? What other homes have had a positive impact on your life? What would you like to duplicate from these homes?

2. As you read Colossians 3, list traits that we must leave out of our homes and traits that we wish to have characterize our homes.

3. Is verbal disrespect or even verbal abuse a problem in your home? What steps will you take to alleviate this problem? Consider writing up a specific plan and asking a friend to pray for you.

4. Is your teen under stress? How can you empathize with her? Do you feel you should intervene or simply encourage?

5. Study your teen. Ask God to make you sensitive to positive steps of growth this week. Praise your teen for her growth in specific areas. Resist the urge to say, "But you can still make progress . . ."

6. What will you do this week to instill a sense of fun into your family life?

Meditate on Philippians 1:9–12. Insert the names of your family members into these verses, making it a prayer for your family.

Bear with each other and forgive whatever grievances you may have against one another. Forgive as the Lord forgave you.

Colossians 3:13

4

Building Good Communication

You just don't understand!

Jeb was not happy. His mother was on his back again about his girlfriend.

"Son, I need to tell you why I'm concerned about your relationship with Ellie."

She told him specific reasons why she did not think this was a healthy relationship. As his mom finished, Jeb stood up, clenched his fists, and struggled for control. He said, "You just don't understand! You don't know everything. You're being unfair. You have to let me make my own decisions."

And he stormed out of the room.

Let's face it. We don't always understand. We don't know everything. Often we are wrong. But we do long to be able to communicate with our kids. We want to stay close in this season in which the tendency will be to grow apart.

Several things will help us lay a foundation for good communication in this tricky season.

Foundations for Good Communication

Develop Sharp Antennae

The Scriptures say, "Be sure you know the condition of your flocks, give careful attention to your herds" (Prov. 27:23). I've found this challenges me to study my children. What are their interests? What are their pressures? What are their fears? What are their dreams? Who are their friends? What are they like? Communication deepens when we know each other.

A car pool is a great research tool. Teens often forget you are there. You hear things you might not hear in a face-to-face conversation. And sometimes it's easier to get someone else's child to talk than it is your own. Car time also provides an opportunity for one-on-one talks. You have a captive audience. And you aren't distracted by the phone, other kids, or tasks. As much as we tire of driving kids all over the place, we lose this *window of connecting* when they get their license.

Other parents can be a resource. Amy's son Ralph is not a talker. When asked, "How was school today?" he replies, "Fine." Period. It's hard for her to know what's really going on in his life. But Amy has an ace in the hole. It's Stacy's mom. Stacy is in the same class with Ralph, and she's a talker. She tells her mother everything. Stacy's mom clues Amy in about what's going on. When Ralph made some strong, thoughtful remarks in English class in defense of the faith, Stacy told her mom, who told Amy. When Ralph started going out with Heather, Stacy's mom told Amy all about

Heather. In a way, Stacy's mom is one of Amy's windows into her son's world.

If we want to understand our kids, we must spend time in their world. Chaperone a field trip. Attend an away game. Walk the halls of their school. Volunteer at their school and get to know the teachers. Read the student newspaper. (You may have to make a special trip to school to get it. They will forget to bring it home!) You'll soon discover issues that your child is faced with. Racial tensions, gay-lesbian pressures, eating disorders, drinking and drugs, gambling, spiritualism, and witchcraft. Realize that the issues change frequently. What was an issue for your eighteen-year-old may be different than what your sixteen-year-old is facing.

Recently I talked with Christin, a youth specialist working with high school students. She told me that the latest trend with high school girls is self-mutilation. It's referred to among teens as "cutting." Girls cut their wrists or legs to release the pain of their depression. While it borders on being "trendy" among some circles of kids, including Christian kids, it is symptomatic of deeper problems that need professional attention. Often we are clueless as to what is going on in our kid's culture and in our kid's life. And we can't afford to be.

Frequently I have prayed, "God, give me sharp antennae. Help me to notice what's going on in my teen's world. Teach me how to study him. Show me his needs. Help me not to miss signals."

Learn When to Speak and When to Remain Silent

One day I was working at my desk. Allison, sixteen, was hanging around me. "Is there anything I can do for you?" I asked her.

"Not really," she responded. But she kept hanging around. I've learned that when teens hang around they usually have something on their minds. And sometimes they need a little help getting it out. Silently asking God to help me be sensitive, I put my pen down and went over to sit on the couch with her.

"How are you feeling about seeing Jay tonight?" I asked. Jay was a boy she'd met at a Christian summer camp six months earlier. He was coming into town and wanted to see her. "Are you a little nervous?"

"Yeah, I guess so," she responded.

"Well, that's normal," I reassured her. "It's awkward to go out with someone you haven't seen in several months, and it's easy to be nervous about keeping the conversation going."

After talking a bit more, I simply put my arms around her and prayed for her time with Jay. Later when she came in, she jumped on our bed and said, "Mom, it worked. We had fun and it was easy to talk to him!"

At seventeen, Fay is not pleasant to live with. Much of what she says is aimed at getting a reaction from her mother. Sitting together in church on Sunday, Fay groaned when the Scriptures were read. Turning to her mom, she said, "I'm sick of all this Bible stuff. I'm just not interested in Christian stuff these days."

Her wise mom did not respond at all. Two hours later at a fellowship luncheon with parents, teens, and youth leaders, Fay was overheard saying to a leader, "I want to be an influence for Christ in my school this year."

Sometimes we need to be silent when our teen makes rash comments.

Eve and her parents had been through two years of major difficulty. Finally she and her parents began seeing a Christian counselor, simply to have a third party help them communicate. One of the hardest pieces of advice the counselor gave Eve's parents was, "You must not react to most of what she says. Not reacting will diffuse the situation. Instead, let her talk, and then respond to her with comments like, 'That's interesting. How do you feel about that?'"

As her parents practiced this, they soon found that Eve talked in circles until she began to listen to herself.

With teenagers we have to begin to listen more and direct less. This can be very hard, especially for parents who are natural problem solvers. Often I have to bite my tongue so I don't offer three quick solutions to fix their problems. After all, it would be so easy if they'd just listen to me. But that's not what they need at the moment. They need a listening, empathetic parent.

It takes a lot of wisdom, a lot of mistakes, and a lot of prayer to figure out when to listen and when to offer advice. But when in doubt, we can just listen. If it seems appropriate, we can ask, "Honey, do you need me to just listen right now, or do you want some advice?" Sometimes we need to let them lead us.

When our teens do want to talk, they need our full attention. We need to turn off the TV (just pushing the mute button isn't enough), put down the paper, get up from the computer, and look them in the eye. This demonstrates respect and communicates that we value their thoughts.

What Do We Do If They Won't Talk?

Relax. Part of becoming independent involves privacy. Teens don't want to tell parents everything. They will be more likely to tell their friends. This lack of communication with your child is hard, especially if you used to be the one your child talked to. But usually it's normal. If, on the other hand, your child is totally withdrawing from family and friends or gravitating to friends with a negative influence, you will need to be alert to potential problems.

It also helps to be creative. Shelly's son Craig isn't as communicative as her other boys. She has found that the best way to get him to talk is by playing a game. So often she'll challenge him to a card game or a Ping-Pong match. She has noticed that if he's engaged in something, he's more likely to talk. And he responds to her playful nature.

"Is there any girl you like?"

Silence.

"That's okay you don't have to tell me. But I'm dying to know, so if I win this round, will you tell me?"

Humor is important in communication. My son John doesn't like it when I ask him for all the details about a party. My husband doesn't like having to give so many details either, but he knows they are important to me, so he struggles to comply. I tell my son, "Hey, I'm training you to be a good husband. Your wife will want details, so practice on me!" And he rolls his eyes and tries to recall the details.

Principles to Communicate

We want to communicate so many principles to our children, and as they hit the teen years we realize we have so little time left. We can't have one talk to communicate our principles and then consider it done. What's important to us will be communicated verbally and nonverbally over the space of a lifetime. And what's important may change. Each of us will have our own unique principles, but included in our list should be the following.

Character Matters

Our culture screams that accomplishments and success are what matter. Being the best. Getting there first. But in the scheme of life character is what matters. Integrity, compassion, respect for others, a servant's heart, joy, self-discipline, and responsibility are just a few character traits we long to have and to see our children develop. Our children will know what traits we value. And they will be quick to point out any hypocrisy on our part.

Do we watch our language at church or Bible study and then let loose at home?

Do I treat the gentleman who cleans my office in the same manner as I treat my business partner? Do I genuinely care for him?

Do I speak to my mate or my child in the same manner as I would my friend?

We must be growing ourselves at the same time that we are training our children. When we fall short, we must admit it and take new steps to grow in that area. Kids respond to a parent who is honest about his or her shortcomings and who is actively seeking to change.

Our failures do not give our teen an excuse to misbehave, even though it's easy for them to say, "After all, my parent does it, why shouldn't I?" However, we cannot fail to recognize that our behavior—or lack of it—will model what character traits we value. And our children will be impacted.

Priorities Count

"Love the Lord your God with all your heart and with all your soul and with all your mind. . . . Love your neighbor as yourself" (Matt. 22:37–39). In this statement, Jesus has given us priorities to live by. My first priority is to love God. Practically speaking, this means taking the time to cultivate my own relationship with Him. If my kids see me regularly on my knees in prayer and regularly studying the Scriptures, they will catch the vision that God is first. If they hear me ask forgiveness, they will know that I acknowledge my sin and want to be forgiven and to grow.

But what if you don't have faith? What if your faith is shaky? Be honest about where you are or are not. And seek to grow yourself. As you grow, share what you are learning with your children. Don't beat them over the head with it. Instead, share it in a manner in which you would share with your best friend. As your faith develops, changes will occur in your home, and it will become evident that personal faith is becoming a top priority.

If your kids see you caring for others—family members, neighbors, anyone in need—they will be more likely to become other-centered instead of self-centered. A friend of mine says there are two types of people in the world. One walks into a room with a "here I am" attitude, waiting for others to cater to her, while another walks into a room with a "there you are" attitude, seeking to care for others. Teens by nature are self-centered, yet if they are consistently challenged to reach out to others and if they see you doing it, they will one day "get it." But don't expect results now. You are building for the future.

The Role of Feelings

"I don't *feel* like going to practice. The coach won't let me play anyway. No matter how hard I work, I still sit on the bench and listen to him yell and curse at all the players. I'm just not going today. I don't need this."

Maybe the coach isn't a good role model. Perhaps he's not fair. But if your child has made a commitment to the team, he should go.

We have to learn that we cannot live life based on feelings. We must learn to do what is right. We know this as adults. How many times have we wanted to run away, to leave our spouse, to give up on our child, to quit work? But we don't because we know it's not right. We do our kids a great disservice if we allow them to let their feelings control their actions. We can validate the feelings. They are important. But then we need to train our child to do what is right.

"I know you are disappointed and frustrated. I am so sorry, and I feel badly too. It's hard to keep going when it's so discouraging, but you made a commitment and you must go."

Resist the parental urge to bail your child out, to talk to the coach and to ask for playing time. The lesson that your child is learning in endurance is far more important than his getting playing time.

Resist the temptation to blame the coach. If your child grows up hearing Mom or Dad blame the teacher, the coach, the friends or lack of friends, the youth group, or the parent that left for his unhappiness, he will quickly learn that his misery is not his fault—it's always someone else's—and he will indeed become an unhappy person. No one and no situation will please him.

Too many well-intentioned parents bail their children out or blame others without realizing that the message the child hears is "I'm not responsible. This is someone else's fault."

The Principle of Waiting

We live in an instant society. Email, instant photos, microwaves, quick-relief medicines, bursting IPOs (initial public offering) in a raging bull market. We like quick results, and we don't like to wait for anything. Even we parents find it so hard waiting for our child to learn obedience, to conquer bad habits, to grow in a positive self-image. Yet waiting is a fact of life, and we do our children a great disservice if we don't teach them to wait at a young age.

So even if you can grant their material wishes, don't do it all. It will not hurt them to wait for that video game, that car. Make them wait to date, to drive others with their new license, to take road trips. We do not need to hurry our kids, pushing them into adulthood before they have the wisdom and experience they will need. Much of life is waiting, and a child who learns the principle of waiting will be more likely to wait for sex until marriage, to wait for that job promotion instead of resorting to white-collar or blue-collar crime to get there faster.

This will not be easy to teach. You will be very unpopular. You will be accused of living in the Dark Ages. But the truth is, you are preparing them for the future. They can't see it now. Don't expect them to.

Decision Making

During these years, our child is making more and more of his own decisions. This is crucial. Often we make one of two mistakes. We hover over them, are too involved and overparent, or we release them too quickly.

Jake's dad is his best friend. He's also his prayer partner and accountability partner. They talk every day. Both love Christ and are seeking to follow him. But Jake at eighteen lacks confidence. He can't make a decision without his dad's input. His dad has been too involved. What Jake needs is for his dad to say, "Son, I have confidence in you. You can make this decision."

If Jake makes a bad decision, he'll learn from it. We all make bad decisions. But we should not become paralyzed in making a decision out of fear of failure. We want to raise decisive kids, and letting them make decisions is a big part of this.

Jane's parents, on the other hand, have given up. They too are strong believers, but seventeen-year-old Jane has pushed them to the limit, so they've "let her go," saying she has to make her own decisions. Many nights they don't know where she is. Often she misses school. Several times they've had to call the police. In their desperation they relinquished crucial decisions and control to an underage child who was not yet ready to make wise decisions.

There are many things we have to consider in determining how much to be involved in our teen's decisions. Their age, their trustworthiness, the past decisions they've made, as well as what this current decision involves are all factors. Often it's a hard call. It helps to ask, "Is this decision going to have lifelong consequences?" Choosing to play baseball instead of basketball isn't a life-determining decision. Let them decide. On the other hand, traveling alone with a girlfriend or boyfriend would be life determining and requires parental involvement. Going to college or taking a job should be a joint decision. (We will look at this challenge more closely in chapter 10.)

We need to be releasing our teens to make their own decisions more and more each year. It should have begun when they were very small with letting them pick out their own clothes. It must continue in the teen years, but it will be harder for us as parents because the stakes are higher. Our kids will make some bad choices and have to live with the consequences. But they will learn from this.

Resolving Conflict

In a house full of teens there is going to be conflict. It's a given. How we work through conflict will depend upon the atmosphere in our home and the relationships we have established.

Carrie was furious because it was prom night and her parents wouldn't let her go to a postprom all-night sleepover at one of the boy's homes.

"You don't trust me! His parents will be there. Nothing will happen. You say I'm growing up and you want me to make my own decisions, but you won't let me. You are just hypocrites! I hate you."

It's best not to react in such situations until you've had a chance to cool off. Words hurt, and it's all too easy in the heat of the moment to say things we will regret later. Teens haven't learned that yet. But we have. So a better option is to say, "Let's take some time to think about this and meet later to discuss it, when you've calmed down."

As you try to resolve such issues, several things will be helpful. You are the parent. You have the authority to say no. You will not be popular for it. Sometimes our kids are relieved when we say no, but they will never admit it. They want freedom, but they still need limits. It's wise to compromise when we can. We will discuss this in more detail in the next chapter, but in resolving conflict the following chart will be helpful for both you and your child. It's also helpful in resolving conflict in marriage.

Conflict Resolution[1]

Focus On:	Rather Than:
One issue	Many issues
The problem	The person
Behavior	Character
Specifics	Generalizations
Expression of feelings	Judgment of character
"I" statements	"You" statements
Observation of facts	Judgment of motive
Mutual understanding	Who's winning or losing

Avoid using the words *always*, *never*, and *everyone*. Don't expect your child to agree with you. She is unlikely to say, "Boy, Dad, you are so wise! I appreciate you." One day in the future you may hear this, but not now.

Anticipating Conflict

It was the week before exams, and I was THE NAG again. My son did not want to talk to me. I was always on his back about studying. I knew his college choice was on the line. And he hadn't opened his books for a crucial exam. It could have lifelong consequences! Now he was in his room strumming his guitar! Nag, nag, nag. Once again it was just a bad week in our relationship. I was on pins and needles. He was withdrawing. The atmosphere in my home was tense. *There has to be a better way*, I said to myself.

It took nagging three children before I finally learned how to anticipate and better handle this exam conflict.

By the time the twins (our fourth and fifth kids) reached high school, I had a plan. Two weeks before exams began, I met with each twin individually to formulate a study calendar. We talked about all of their courses. Which one would they need to study for the most? Which one needed less time? Looking at the exam schedule, we drew up a study calendar with study times for each subject beginning that very week. Together we filled it out. Their first exam season, I monitored how they were doing and encouraged them in sticking to the plan and in making adjustments as we went along. Having a written-out plan that they posted in their room eliminated much of my nagging. It also helped them to feel more in control of their schedule and less overwhelmed. The next semester I gave them a date by which I wanted their study plan finished. I held them to the date. They worked it out by themselves and then went over it with me. We made some adjustments. The third semester I merely asked them for the schedule by a certain date and prayed for them.

A simple, three-part lesson in training has worked well for us:

1. I do it with them.
2. They do it and I check it.
3. They do it, share it with us, and we pray.

Today as college students they, on their own initiative, draw up their exam study plan. No, I don't see it; they just call and tell us how to pray.

Sometimes anticipating conflict and preparing a strategy will help alleviate tension. Often we have to blow it with one child to learn how to handle an issue with another.

Communicating in Times of Pain

At sixteen, Valerie was in pain. Her mom and dad were getting a divorce. It was a nasty situation. Each parent wanted her to live with him or her. But Valerie chose to go with her mom to a city thousands of miles away. It was hard on both of them. The culture was so different; they were lonely and depressed.

Valerie's homesickness overwhelmed her, and she confessed to her mom that she needed to go back home to be with friends in a familiar setting. Valerie returned home to live with her dad. This devastated her mom. Although she was a believer, her former husband was not. She feared that without her, there would be no Christian influence in her daughter's life. She knew she had to keep communication open with Valerie. And so she made a decision to write to her daughter every single day. Some days she wrote just a few lines: "I'm thinking about you today. There's no news here except that I love you." Other days she had more to say. Much time would pass without any response. Valerie's mom says, "It was a time of giving up control but not of giving up my prayers. In my letters I tried to tell her things about me rather than prying into her life. This made it easier for her to respond."

In time, Valerie's anger at life began to dissipate, and a new communication began between mother and daughter. They began to share common interests like recipes. Slowly they are building an adult friendship by mail. And Valerie is sharing more personally with her mom.

Valerie's mom gives us a good example. Sometimes all we can do is be intentional in communicating and pray, pray, pray.

Conflict doesn't always get resolved. It can be messy. It may end in an impasse. Our child may be angry. We may feel like a failure. Yet no matter what the issue is, there is one thing we have that our child doesn't—perspective. Perspective comes with age and experience. And perspective enables us to give them hope.

It might help to say to them or to write in a note, "Honey, we're having a hard time right now. We don't understand each other. We hurt one another. But I want you to know that I love you and am committed to you forever. We will come through this time. We will be friends one day. I have the confidence that God will use this for good in both of our lives."

Focus Questions

Meditate on 2 Timothy 1, the letter Paul wrote to his young friend Timothy.

1. How would you describe the tone of this letter? What characterizes Paul's words?
2. How would you describe your communication with your teen? In which areas would you like to see improvement?

3. Make a list of principles that are important to you. How will you communicate each principle to your teen? Include both nonverbal and verbal ways of communication.

4. Take time this week to study your teen (see Prov. 27:23). Ask God to give you sharp antennae so that you will be able to sense things you need to know. Write down what you observe about your teen. What has God revealed to you that will strengthen your understanding of your teen and enhance your communication?

Meditate on 2 Timothy 2. Highlight the principles Paul wanted to communicate to Timothy.

For God has not given us a spirit of timidity, but a spirit of power, of love and of self-discipline.

2 Timothy 1:7

5

Setting Limits and Letting Go

Why can't you just trust me?

"Mom, I'm going over to Alice's house tonight. They have a new hot tub, and we're all going to try it out."

"Who is Alice and where does she live?" Roy's mom responded.

"She's this new girl at school. She's really smart. You'd like her."

"Will her parents be there?" his mom continued.

"I guess so. Stop asking so many questions. Everything will be fine. Why can't you just trust me?"

For parents, a statement like this makes us feel like dirt. It's as if we are being accused of negating the core essence of our child's personal value. The failure must be ours. We falter. We become defensive. We stumble with a weak response, "I do trust you, but . . ."

Trust issues crop up in so many areas with our teens. They want our trust. They usually deserve it. Yet often they throw us an issue dressed in a trust wrapper that is about a lot more than just trust.

Sometimes a better response would be, "This issue is not about trust. It's about wisdom and experience."

"Son," you might say, "suppose I had to have a serious operation. Would you want a brilliant, second-year medical student to perform the operation or a surgeon who's been in practice for several years? I hope you'd choose the experienced surgeon. He'd be more likely to recognize potential problems and avoid them or correct them. Even if the med student is in the top of his class, is sincere, is a strong believer, and has impeccable character, you'd still choose the experienced surgeon. The student's good intentions can't replace experience. It's the surgeon's experience, his resumé, that enables you to put your trust in him."

In a similar way, parental wisdom and experience may lead us to say no even though our child's intentions are good.

If I had to write a formula for trust, it would be: Trust = Wisdom + Experience (demonstrated responsibility over a period of time). Proverbs 22:3 says, "A prudent [wise] man sees danger and takes refuge, but the simple keep going and suffer for it."

At seventeen Fay thinks she's mature. To her, mature means *I'm old enough to do what I want.* But in her "maturity," she's rude to her parents, not much interested in anyone but herself, irresponsible, inconsiderate of others, and tends to flirt with danger. Yes, there are some signs of growth, but she's not yet mature. She has not yet demonstrated that she's trustworthy in many areas. She has yet to build a resumé of making responsible choices.

"But everyone else gets to . . ." Often this statement goes hand in hand with, "You don't trust me." It makes us feel like the most unreasonable parents in town. We have to realize that this is rarely true. We may be in the minority, but we are unlikely to be "the only one who . . ." Yet, even if we are the *only* parents who don't let our teen do something, we still have to do what we believe is best for our child. We are not running for most popular parent. And it's not what our child thinks of us now that's nearly as important as what she will think of us twenty years from now. We have to keep this long-range perspective.

How do we move past the feeling of being on the defense to a more positive offensive strategy?

We need a strategy that will enable us to set reasonable limits while letting our teens go. The following strategy points are important to understand before we can deal effectively with the hot topics.

Strategy One: Avoid Two Extremes

When I was growing up, I loved to climb up on a seesaw with a friend. If we weighed approximately the same, it wasn't hard to position ourselves so we could balance in midair. But if our weight differences were significant, it took some moving around to achieve balance. One of us might have to move up, while the other might have to slide back. We had to avoid being too extreme, or one end would come crashing to the ground, bouncing the other person off the top side. How thrilled we were when we found just the right spots to sit in order to hang together, suspended in midair.

Discipline in the family can be a bit like riding a seesaw.

On each end of the seesaw there are two extremes we need to avoid: *the religion of self-esteem* and *the religion of regulations*.

We buy into the *religion of self-esteem* when we believe that "making sure our child feels good about himself" is our most important goal. To ensure that our child is happy, we give in to his demands. We can't bear for him to be miserable, to feel sad. Discipline is difficult for us. Perhaps we were raised in a strict, legalistic home. No matter what we did, it never seemed good enough. Perhaps there was verbal or physical abuse. In an attempt not to repeat what was done to us, we placate our child. If our child feels strongly about something, we give in. We don't seem to be able to follow through with punishments. It's just too unpleasant. Our spouse may have left. Our child may have had some hard knocks, and we feel sorry for him. "I just can't discipline him; he's had such a hard time" becomes our excuse. The result of this religion will be an insecure child, because the child, not the parents, is calling the shots in the home.

At the opposite end of the seesaw is the *religion of regulations*. Your teen hits the door after school. You immediately become Drill Sergeant Mom or Dad.

"Get up to your room and clean it up! Then practice your piano and do your homework. Find your tennis shoes so you will be ready for practice. Lay out your clothes for tomorrow."

We issue orders right and left. We overdose on making sure that our child behaves properly at all times. We seem to be continuously on his back and rarely have time simply to enjoy him. The result of this religion will be an insecure child, because he will feel that no matter what he does, he can never measure up.

Recognize which end of the seesaw you most likely fall onto, and take steps to balance your style. Often two parents will tend toward opposite ends. This can be a source of marital conflict as you try to raise your teens. Or it can help you balance each other. When you need to balance on the seesaw, you have to move closer to one another. This holds true in marriage as well. Parenting teens can cause conflict in a good marriage and further damage a troubled relationship. But it doesn't have to. Take steps to guard your marriage and move closer to each other. Get help from a wise older couple or a counselor. You may find that as you work through this tough parenting issue of avoiding extremes for the sake of your child, you learn problem-solving techniques that will benefit your marriage. A mutual concern over a child can be a blessing for a troubled marriage because it gives you a common concern to work out.

No matter which end of the seesaw we fall onto, it's crucial to recognize the goal of our discipline. We want our child to learn *self-discipline*. This grows out of discipline. But we also want our child to learn to obey his earthly parents, whose voices he hears say, "I love you," whose arms he feels give him hugs, in order that as he grows he will be weaned from obeying us to obeying his heavenly Father, whose voice he might not audibly hear, whose arms he won't exactly feel, yet who he has been taught loves him even more than we do. How can he learn to obey Him if he hasn't learned to obey us?

Strategy Two: Separate Swing Issues from Crucial Issues

I was nearly asleep when I heard whispering in the hall and then an unmistakable bumping sound, interspersed with giggles, coming from the stairs. *What is going on?* I wondered. I knew our son John was due in from youth group and that his sister Allison had driven to get him. As the noise increased, I knew something strange was definitely up. Bracing myself for a "teenage unknown," I staggered out into the hall to see what was happening. Four teens were trying to get the dirtiest couch I had ever seen up the stairs into the boys' room. Our two sons have grown up in one nine-by-ten-foot bedroom. There's hardly any unused space.

"What are you doing with that?" I asked.

"Mom, it's our new couch!" John responded joyfully. "I found it on the street during a treasure hunt. Someone put it out for trash, but I thought it would be perfect for our room."

"But it's filthy!" I exclaimed. "Who knows what diseases and bugs are in it? And it doesn't even have cushions. You can't put that gross thing in your room!"

"Mom," my son said in a serious voice, albeit with a twinkle in his eye, "this is my teenage rebellion. Be grateful!"

He got me on that, and the couch was moved into an already crowded bedroom, where it lived as a monument to "his rebellion" for the next three years. Its presence reminded me of an important principle for parents of teens: Distinguish between crucial issues and swing issues.

Crucial issues are those issues that have to do with character. Integrity, compassion, responsibility, respect, self-discipline. Crucial issues are also those on which the Bible has clear teaching. Sex outside of marriage, murder, stealing. Our laws would also constitute crucial issues. Our law says it's illegal to drink if you are under twenty-one. When we determine how to handle an issue, we consider the crucial issues as nonnegotiables. Lying isn't tolerated. It's a nonnegotiable.

Swing issues, on the other hand, aren't always so cut-and-dried. It isn't as clear how to handle them. Trendy dress, earrings, belly rings, nose rings, blue hair, tattoos, messy rooms, moodiness, movies, parties, nasty couches. When should I stand firm and when can I let go? There are no easy answers, but there are some guidelines.

Boys with earrings can be offensive to a baby boomer. I need to get over my bias. I don't have to like it, but I must not make this a crucial issue.

When our boys expressed interest in getting an ear pierced, I said, "Fine, but if you do, I'll get a nose ring!"

They knew there was a chance I just might, and they weren't willing to risk that embarrassment, so they didn't pierce their ears.

When Liza got her belly button pierced, her very proper mom responded, "Oh, Liza, that's *soo* trashy!" And both mother and daughter dissolved into fits of laughter. It's a swing issue.

Sometimes there's a gray line between a swing and crucial issue. What about your teen's room? Doesn't keeping your room clean have to do with character? After all, it's self-discipline, it's responsibility. True, but with teens we have to have places that we, the parents, give in. When our kids were small, we tried to train them by insisting that they keep their rooms clean. But now in these teen years, this is an area in which we can loosen up. Simply shut their door. Remember the stresses of academics, relationships, and college choice pressures that they are under. One day they will remember the importance of a neat room. Let their future roommate deal with this. This is a gray line. It will not harm them or someone else.

When our children are young, we should be very firm. But as they reach the teen years, we have to loosen up where we can. It's the swing issues that provide us with opportunities to loosen up. If we don't loosen up on some swing issues, we will fall into the religion of regulations, and our teens will be less likely to hear us on the crucial issues.

What do we do when issues seem to cross the gray line from swing to crucial? This is an important question. We have to define the line.

All teens are moody. Especially girls. Usually ignoring the moodiness of a teen is the most effective means of handling it. But if the moodiness persists for a couple of weeks and seems to be having a negative impact on the atmosphere of the family, we need to deal with it.

When Allison was a teen, she had typical mood swings, which we tended to ignore. But at one point she seemed to stay cross, moody, and rude to her siblings for a couple of weeks. Mealtimes weren't fun. Her disposition was putting a cloud over the atmosphere in our home. Our whole family was being held hostage by a moody teen over a period of time. The line had been crossed.

Johnny and I decided that he was the best one to take her aside and have a talk about the impact her attitude was having on the family. He chose a time to take her out and discuss this with her. We talked together about how he should do this. He shared with her how proud he was of her in so many areas. He reassured her that he understood how hard it was to be a teen, and he gave her hope that we would come through this time together. He also explained to her what we were observing about her moodiness and the influence she was having on the family. He prayed with her about the changes that needed to take place. No, she didn't respond, "Dad, you are so right!" She was fairly quiet during the conversation. No, he didn't feel like it was a great talk. But we did begin to see changes.

In the preceding chapter I told about a counselor advising Eve's parents to remain quiet and not respond to her comments. Wise advice—unless the comments begin to cross the line.

"Life stinks; the teacher's a turkey; you are so unfair" are comments that can be ignored sometimes. But when they become "You b——; you stupid so-and-so," they have crossed the line to verbal disrespect and thus have become a crucial issue. Swift, firm punishment must be enforced. It's a character issue. This kind of back talk cannot be tolerated—ever.

As you seek to define the line, ask the following: Is this a character issue? Does it have the potential to have a long-term negative impact on my child or on someone else? Is this a place I can loosen up even if I don't want to?

Strategy Three: Determine When and How to Negotiate

Why are we so afraid to say no? When should we say no, and when should we negotiate? These are important questions for parents of teens.

Don't Negotiate Crucial Issues

As mentioned earlier, these are nonnegotiable; they have to do with character, with biblical teaching, with obeying the law. Lying is not acceptable, ever. But let's get picky. Your child insists that "technically" she didn't lie about where she really was. She just didn't tell you everything. She shouldn't be punished because she didn't really lie. Wait a minute. Did she seek to deceive? Lying in its rawest form is an attempt to deceive. She's guilty.

Our kids must learn that "no" means "no" and not "maybe, if you throw a temper tantrum, whine, or threaten to run away." It will be difficult if they did not learn this when they were young. If they have been subtly calling the shots and manipulating their parents, change will be hard and will take longer. But it is never too late to do what is right. For the sake of your child and your family, you must be firm. Your child needs the security of knowing that he isn't in control. That you mean what you say. That your word is good.

Do Negotiate Whenever You Can

Your daughter is spending too much time on the phone. Homework isn't getting done. No one else can use the phone. She isn't getting enough sleep. What should you do? It's time to negotiate with her. Pick a good time to chat. Not right when she gets off the phone or when she's in the midst of studying. Say, "We have a situation that we need to solve together. We need for you to cut back on your phone time on school nights." Give her your reasons, then finish with, "How would you suggest that we do this?"

See if you can come up with an agreeable plan together. If you can't, you are the parent and you will have to enforce a plan. But it's far better if you can negotiate one together.

How you approach the issue is key. Don't attack the person (the child). Attack the issue (the phone). Be respectful. Talk to her as you would a colleague.

Do Research and Get the Facts

"There's a party Friday night at Joe's. Everyone is going. Can I go?"

Before you say yes or no, it's best to get the facts. Will Joe's parents be there? Do you know Joe's parents? Will alcohol be served? What will be happening at the party? (i.e., will movies be shown? If so, which ones?) What time is it over? Who is your child going with?

Finding out the facts may necessitate a call to Joe's mom or dad, a talk with other parents, and research on a movie to be shown. Taking the time to find out the facts will be inconvenient for a busy parent. Do it anyway. We'll discuss handling friends and their parents further in chapter 7, but your first responsibility is to find out the details.

Often children will hit you with a request for which they "just have to have an answer right now." Teens don't plan ahead. Don't be pressured into having to make a decision right now. Instead, say, "Son, if you have to know right this minute, the answer will be no. If you can wait until I have a chance to talk to your dad (or another parent) and find out some information, you might get an answer that you will like better."

Be United as a Couple

Our children learn at a young age which parent to go to with a request. It's vital that parents of teens present a united front. Otherwise, the child is going to go to the most lenient parent and ignore the stricter parent. Make a commitment, especially if you are the lenient parent, to say, "I have to discuss this first with your father [or mother or another couple]." If you are a single parent, have someone to whom you can go for advice.

You may have many more discussions with each other about child-raising issues than you'd like as parents of teens. Be encouraged—it is a brief season, and God will use what can be difficult discussions to help you grow in your marriage. It will be helpful to develop a discipline strategy together as your children approach the teen years. It should be a strategy that you can work from and make changes to as necessary.

Communicate Expectations Clearly

"Be sure your homework is finished before you leave for practice. Come straight home after practice; it's a school night. Have a great practice!"

It's our responsibility to be sure we have communicated clearly with our teen. If there is any chance of a miscommunication, write your expectations out and post them. We will have times when we miscommunicate, but we can avoid much of this by writing one another notes. Notes help to eliminate parental nagging. Teens can have selective memories. If they are likely to forget a chore or a request, stick a Post-it note on their mirror as a friendly reminder.

Have Specific Consequences for Misbehavior and Follow Through with Punishment

It's far more important to have a few rules that you consistently enforce than lots of rules that you are inconsistent in enforcing. If you don't follow through to enforce your discipline policy, your unintentional message to your child is, "Your actions have no value; they don't really matter because they don't have consequences." Ouch—that's not what we intended to communicate, but that is the ultimate message.

This scenario will be particularly true for the parent who tends toward the religion of self-esteem. The reality is that if you don't follow through with punishment, you are undermining your child's self-esteem instead of building it.

Make Sure the Punishment Fits the Infraction and Enforce It

Your daughter is thirty minutes late keeping curfew. You respond, "That's it, you're grounded for a month."

The truth of the matter is that her grounding will likely last only for a couple of days, until you need her to run errands for you, or until she has an opportunity to do something you want her to do. And the grounding goes out the window.

A more reasonable punishment might be having to be in an hour earlier than her regular curfew next weekend. Stick to it no matter what.

But what if she habitually abuses curfews? Design a plan with your spouse or, if you are a single parent, with another couple. Write it out. "The next time you are late ... will happen. The second time ... will happen." And so forth.

Be sure it is something reasonable that you will enforce. It will be inconvenient for you. But in the long run your inconvenience pales in comparison to the importance of your child learning that actions have consequences.

Let Them Fail and Pray They Get Caught— Don't Bail Them Out

Our son Chris and his friend Nate were making mud balls behind a dirt bank. They decided it would be fun to throw them at passing cars. With a great heave my son let the first ball fly, and it landed smack on the front window of a city police car! Bringing his car to a screeching stop, the cop jumped out, grabbed these two thoroughly frightened boys, and brought them to my front door.

When I opened the door and heard the policeman's explanation of what had happened, it was all I could do not to smile. God had answered my prayer! You see, we've always prayed that if any of our children were doing anything wrong, they'd get caught.

The boys were given a serious lecture about an accident they could have caused, they were grounded for the weekend, and they had to write the officer a thank-you note for catching them. They learned that actions have consequences and that they were lucky to be caught even though they didn't like it at the time.

We can't always be watching our teens like we did our toddlers. Our teens are not always in sight. And it's scary. But we can pray for God to catch them in their wrongdoing. Just recently Ray was driving friends on the New Jersey Turnpike. He was speeding. It "just happened" that his mom's friend was traveling on this busy road at the same time and saw him. She pulled up beside him and shook her finger at him to slow him down. He was humiliated to have been caught by his mother's friend, but he slowed down.

When your child gets caught, don't bail him out. If your daughter plagiarizes on a paper and gets caught and given a bad grade, don't intervene. It's far more crucial that she learn that actions have consequences than that she keep up her GPA while continuing down a path of dishonesty. It's a crucial issue, and we negate its significance if we bail our child out.

Encourage Them to Make Their Own Decisions

"I can't decide whether to try out for the cheerleading squad or the cross-country team," your daughter agonizes. You might ask her what the pros and cons are for each team, but be sure you don't make the decision for her. Instead, say, "You can make this decision. I have confidence in you."

Part of becoming confident and trustworthy involves making choices. Releasing your kids involves letting them make more and more choices. But what if they make a poor choice? They will. So will you. It's part of learning. When you are in the process of letting them go, increase the freedom of choice you give them *in safe areas.* Letting our young teen choose whether or not to attend a party where adults are not present isn't wise. It's dangerous. On the other hand, don't make decisions for them they should be making themselves. It's helpful to ask yourself, "Does this decision involve safety or moral issues?" Slowly and steadily increase the number and importance of decisions you turn over to them.

Remind Them: We're Not Enemies; We're on the Same Team

As you negotiate limits, remind your child that you are his teammate in walking through these teen years. You are not his enemy nor he yours, even though he may feel that at times. You both want what is best for him.

Letting go is a gradual process. It's not eighteen and you're free, whoopee! We both have to be patient. A father said to his daughter, "You want to be independent, but the way you are going about trying to be independent is not right. Our job is to help you become independent in the right way." As they continued to talk, he reaffirmed his love for her and his confidence in her.

Say Yes As Often As Possible

We'd had out-of-town company all week. I was exhausted from playing tour guide in the city. Plus, I had an article that was past due, bills that were unpaid, a dirty house, and stacks of laundry piled up. All I really wanted was for somebody to send me to my room to take a nap!

As I contemplated my desires, the twins burst into the room. "Mom, we want to have a bunch of friends over tomorrow night. Would that be okay?"

Everything in me wanted to say no! But I knew that this was something I should say yes to. In a season when we have to say no many times, we must take care to say yes as often as we can. Saying yes may mean saying no to our own desires, to postponing our own plans. When we say no to a toddler, it does not carry the emotional weight that saying no to a teen carries. Saying yes as often as we can will ease the disappointment of the necessary no's.

This past Easter the twins brought home a dozen of their college friends for the weekend. Easter lunch has always been a big deal to me. I like using my fine china, linen mats, decorating the antique family dining-room table, and having a meal in which we all sit down together.

I had everything all fixed for a gorgeous celebration when we got home from church.

"Gosh, Mom, it's so unseasonably warm. Is there any way we can have a picnic outside?" Susy asked.

I started to respond, "My elegant Easter luncheon a picnic? No way!" But then I remembered: Say yes whenever you can. Not wanting to turn a nice luncheon into a buffet, yet wanting to say yes, I had an idea. "Okay, let's just move the dining room outside!"

We gathered everyone and picked up the oriental rug and the dining-room table and chairs. We moved the whole party, candlesticks and all, to the front yard, where we had a most unusually elegant Easter luncheon. Now, weather permitting, Mom's outdoor dining room has become an Easter tradition.

Be Quick to Say You Were Wrong

I can't count the number of times I have had to say to my teens, "I'm sorry. I was wrong. Will you forgive me?" And I can't remember a time when I *felt* like saying this. Most often I wanted to add, "But if you had or if you hadn't . . ." Usually I am embarrassed. After all, I'm the mom. Yet I have learned to go to my husband and to my kids asking their forgiveness, not because I feel like it, but because God has told me to. We go out of conviction and obedience, not out of feeling. Often there are hurts that will take time to be healed. But the healing cannot begin until we go to one another asking for and granting forgiveness.

Recently I got irritated with Libby. I blamed her for something that was not completely her fault. Everything in my day seemed to have gone wrong. I was tired. And my tongue got the better of me. I knew I needed to apologize. No, I didn't want to. After all, I'm the mother, and she had some fault in the matter. But in this case it was predominantly my problem. Knowing that I had to set things straight, I went to her room.

"Libby," I began, "I shouldn't have said what I did, and I need to ask you to forgive me. I am so sorry. Will you forgive me?"

"Oh, Mom," she replied, "yes, I will forgive you, but thanks for asking."

Healing begins when we humble ourselves and go to one another asking for forgiveness.

Focus Questions

Meditate on Joel 2:12–14.

1. What does Joel encourage the children of Israel to do? How does he portray God's character?
2. On which end of the seesaw, the religion of regulations or the religion of self-esteem, do you tend to lean the most? What has contributed to this? Where is your spouse on the seesaw? How can you use this to balance one another rather than cause friction?
3. Develop a discipline strategy. List your swing issues and your crucial issues. Remember crucial issues have to do with character, with clear biblical teaching, and with obeying the law. They are nonnegotiable. Swing issues are negotiable. How will you communicate your family policy on these issues? What will be your consequences (punishments) for disobedience the first time? The second time?

It is important to write your policy out and then make adjustments as necessary. This should be done with your spouse. A single parent should work in conjunction with a couple, preferably one whose children are close in age to hers or his. It can be helpful to share this policy-making in a group.

Meditate on Psalm 78:1–8. What guidance does the psalmist give about training your children? How might these words impact you this week?

> Return to the LORD your God
>   for he is gracious and compassionate,
> slow to anger and abounding in love.
>
>   Joel 2:13

6

Handling the "Hot Topics"

Help! How should I handle . . . ?

"Your curfew isn't fair . . . I know what you believe [about sex] . . . But I *have* studied . . . Everyone else gets to go see it; it's not what you think . . . This is the twenty-first century—*your* music's old fashioned . . . But I really *need* it; I'll pay you back . . . One drink won't hurt; you're overreacting . . . I *know* how to drive . . . Leave me alone—I don't want to talk about it. Just trust me."

Simply reading these phrases can make us slump into depression because there is no way we can "win." As parents we are on a collision course. C. S. Lewis once said, "Being brought up, no matter how graciously done, is bound to offend."

Handling the hot topics is going to offend. Even in the closest parent-child relationship, there will be times of great unpleasantness. For us as parents, the pain will be twofold; we want our kids to like us, and we don't always know if we are making the right decision. It helps to realize that we will make wrong decisions. We are only human. Yet God can redeem any mistake, any failure. In the pain of the moment, we must also remember that our goal is not to keep our kids liking us. Our ultimate goal is to raise responsible adults with a fervent love for Christ.

As we consider the hot topics, it's important to recognize that these topics are not handled in one conversation with our child. These are fluid issues that will necessitate ongoing conversations prior to the teen years and even beyond them.

If you have flipped to this section hoping to get quick answers for your hot topic with your child, you will likely be frustrated—this chapter will not solve everything for you. Teens are wonderfully complicated children of God, and so are their parents. There is not one quick fix for a teen or for a teen's parents. How you handle your hot issues will be directly influenced by your relationship with your child. This relationship has been shaped by the atmosphere in your home, developed through your communications, and influenced by the limits and the patterns of letting go that you have already begun to establish. So if you have turned to this chapter first seeking a quick solution, it might be wise to go back and read the preceding chapters first. They will help you lay a solid foundation for your relationship with your teen so you can work through the hot topics together. Quick fixes rarely work anyway!

The following seven hot topics are by no means all-inclusive. There are many more. This is also not the final word on these issues. You will differ in your response to some statements, and you will have other helpful, creative approaches yourselves. No one person has the ultimate wisdom on how to handle these complicated issues. Study God's Word, seek the counsel of an older believing couple, and pray, pray, pray. God loves your teen more than you do, and He is your partner in parenting.

Here we go!

Sex

She was gorgeous. Thick jet-black hair and large blue eyes. But as we talked those eyes filled with tears.

"I went further physically than I ever should have with an old boyfriend. We broke up long ago, and now I'm in love with a wonderful guy with firm standards. But I'm so ashamed of my past. I just wish someone had talked to me about limits."

"What about your parents?" I asked. "Did they talk with you about sex?"

"They told me the facts at a young age, but that was pretty much it. Even though they were strong Christians, they didn't really give me any guidelines on things like how far I could go in a dating relationship. I guess it was too awkward for them to talk about. But I wish I had had somebody to talk with."

Talking to our teens about sex will be awkward, difficult, and embarrassing. Most often they don't *want* to talk about it, and we don't know *how* to talk about it. Yet talk we must, and not just one talk explaining the facts of life. It's many talks over many years. After all, our kids are bombarded with sex on every front. Sex isn't an isolated subject. It has to do with commitment, marriage, having children. We and our kids long for intimacy, and kids often think sex is intimacy. It isn't. It's much more. How we handle the hot topic of sex will influence how we handle dating and curfews. As we deal with this explosive topic, a few things will be helpful.

Be Positive

God loves sex! He created it for our mutual pleasure with our mates as well as for having children. Our culture depicts it either as dirty, naughty, sleazy, kinky, exotic, free-for-all, or simply as "no big deal." If we're sexy, we're desirable. If we're desirable, we're worth something.

But God says, "I formed you in your mother's womb. You are fearfully and wonderfully made" (Ps. 139:13–14 paraphrased). Being sexy in the world's eyes is nothing compared to being made in God's eyes. The act of sexual intercourse is a gift. It's not dirty. Instead, it's the most intimate expression of love that God has created for a man and a woman. It's so sacred that He likened it to His being one with us, His body the church. Physically becoming one is a holy moment. Giving yourself to another in the act of love is a gift—a gift God intended a man and a woman to give to each other in marriage.

In a world that cheapens sex, we need to elevate it. We must make sure we communicate its goodness to our children. Explain that this is the greatest wedding present your child can give to his or her mate on their honeymoon. It is so precious it should be treasured and saved until that moment. It is far too precious to be given to anyone else.

As you talk to your child, it's helpful to say, "Son, talking about this is awkward for both of us. But we'll do lots of talking about this over the years. I want you to feel free to ask me any question. No question is dumb. I've had a lot of dumb questions in my years." Then laugh at yourselves. Humor alleviates tension.

Set Standards Based on God's Word

As our kids grow up, they will need to know more of God's standards and the whys behind them. Just like my young friend, they long for clear parameters. And parameters need to be reinforced and reiterated. Remember, our kids are hearing the world's standards over and over again.

Take your kids to God's Word and show them what His standards are. His teaching on some issues leaves room for different interpretations. But in the area of sexual purity He is clear. It's a nonnegotiable.

- He created us to become one flesh with one person (Matt. 19:4–6). We are to remain virgins until we are married and then remain faithful to that one mate.
- Homosexuality is not God's plan (Rom. 1:24–28). Yes, He loves those who are gay, and we should too. But they are not living in accordance with His will. He can and is bringing healing to many who repent and seek Him.[1]
- "It is good for a man not to touch a woman," Paul says in 1 Corinthians 7:1.[2] In the original Greek, touch translates "light a fire within her." So how far can we go physically? A good guideline: Don't ignite the fire of passion. Anything beyond holding hands, kissing, and hugging prior to marriage should be off-limits

for all, and for some even these things may be too much.

- Flee from sexual immorality (1 Cor. 6:18). We must avoid people and places that will be tempting.

Find Creative Ways to Communicate

When each of our children were about twelve, we took them away for a weekend and listened to the tape series "Preparing for Adolescence" by James Dobson.[3] Johnny took the boys. I took the girls. The tapes cover everything from peer pressure to sexual purity. We ate junk food, shopped, and reacted to the tapes together. It helped to have a third party doing the talking. Dennis and Barbara Rainey have prepared a new set, "Passport to Purity," which is excellent.[4]

When our twins, Susy and Libby, were young teens, Johnny took each of them on a special date with a private ceremony. He talked to each about how special she was, highlighting the unique ways she blessed him. He shared with her again God's love for her. He spoke of his pride in her and his prayer that one day God would give her a godly husband who would love and cherish her. And he talked again of God's gift of oneness expressed in sexual union. A gift that God intended to be given only to her husband on her wedding night. He asked her to promise to wait until that night to give this special gift to the man she would one day love even more than her dad. In prayer with her dad, she made this promise to God. Then he gave her a tiny gold key with a gold heart on a necklace. This symbolized that her heart belonged to her dad until the wedding night, when she would give this key to her husband. Today, when the girls wear their necklaces, it serves as a reminder to a promise made to an earthly father who loves them and to a heavenly Father who will enable them to keep their promise.[5]

We have found it helpful to challenge couples who are seriously dating or engaged to sign a purity covenant. The covenant includes Scriptures from Acts 24:16; 1 Corinthians 6:18–20; and 1 Thessalonians 4:3–8, with the following: *In obedience to God's command, I promise to protect your moral purity from this day until marriage. Because I respect and honor you, I commit to build up the inner person of your heart rather than violate you. I pledge to show my love for you in ways that allow both of us to maintain a clear conscience before God and each other.*[6]

Even if the couple has already had sexual relationships, they can confess their sin and receive God's forgiveness. Yes, there will be scars and regrets they will carry for life. However, there is nothing that God can't forgive (1 John 1:9). In signing the covenant, they will begin a fresh relationship with God that will bring great blessing to their own relationship. It is never too late to do what is right.

Communicate Confidence

You may be asking yourself, *How can I hold my children to God's standard when I had sex before marriage? What do I tell them?* We hold them to God's standard because that is His best for them and for us. It communicates confidence in them and in God. Even if you didn't keep it, it does not mean that your children can't. How much you tell them about your past depends upon your relationship with them. It's always best to tell the truth. You may feel it would be helpful to share the pain that your disobedience to God has caused you. You do not need to give details.

Our kids need to know that we have confidence in them. One mom, a strong believer aware of the temptations and of the dangers of AIDS, told her son that he should not have sex before he was married, but that if he couldn't resist, he should wear a good condom. The son, a believer, was a bit horrified at his mom's comment. What she unintentionally communicated to her son was that she didn't really believe he would be able to wait.

Allison, our eldest, recalls a talk I had with her when she began to date. "Sweetie," I said, "I want you to know that there will come a time when you will be overwhelmed with physical passion for a guy. You may be shocked by how strong it is. This is not bad. It is a gift from God, a promise of what you have to look forward to in marriage. It's a passion that you will have to hold in check until you are married. It will be hard, but you can do it."

When our son Chris became engaged, a friend who was already married encouraged him to remain pure. "This is something you can do," Mark said. "Yes, it's hard as all get out, but you can do it." Mark's words were encouraging in a culture that screams, "It's impossible!"

But what if it's too late? It's never too late from God's perspective. That's why there is forgiveness. Even if your child is already having sex, it's never too late for him or her to ask for forgiveness, to become "new." The prophet Ezekiel says, "I will give you a new heart and put a new spirit in you; I will remove from you your heart of stone and give you a heart of flesh" (Ezek. 36:26). How you handle this situation will depend upon your relationship with your child. But always give your child the gift of hope. We will look at handling a difficult situation involving pregnancy in chapter 9.

Utilize Resources

Today there are many good resources available to us as we talk with our kids. The video *Let's Talk about It* by youth workers Ash and Eva Ashburn is an excellent resource for senior high students.[7] I showed it to a roomful of teens and postteens at my house and asked for their feedback. Sometimes it's easier to show something like this to a group rather than just your own child. It's much less awkward, and the response is likely to be better. They liked it, and one girl took a copy to show to a high school Bible study she was leading!

Other people will be invaluable in helping us. Our kids are at an age when they need to hear truth from someone other than Mom or Dad.

I will be forever grateful to our youth minister, Jeff, who for years had my boys in a discipleship group. They talked about sex, dating, pornography, and many other hot topics. And the boys listened. Why? It wasn't Mom or Dad.

If you have experienced any form of sexual abuse, you may need help in communicating with your teens. Your experience is not your fault. There is healing. An excellent book, *The Wounded Heart*, by Dr. Dan Allender will be encouraging. But you also need to work this through with a godly counselor.

Pray for Your Child in This Area

Amy was going through a rebellious season—running with a fast crowd, drinking, and dating a jerk (in her parents' opinion). When she was young, she'd given her life to Christ, but lately she'd put her faith on the shelf. Now she was involved in a very physical relationship, and she decided that it was going to be okay for her to "go all the way" with her boyfriend. She figured "it" would happen after a party the following weekend, and she was ready. For many months her mom had cried and prayed over this child. There wasn't anything left to say. It had all been said. But she never stopped praying. The date night finally came, but to Amy's amazement her boyfriend chose *this* night to break up with her. Months later, after God had brought about many changes in Amy's life, she said to her mom, "God really took charge that scary night. I guess He heard your prayers."

Another young couple was parking and into heavy petting. A "fire" had been lit and was about to explode, when a cop pulled up and knocked on the window!

Pray for breakups, pray for your child to get caught, pray for "cool," godly role models who will speak the truth. Pray for your child's future spouse, that God would protect him or her physically, and pray for the parents who are raising him or her.

Dating and Curfews

When should I let my child date? What if I don't like the date? And anyway, what is dating? Is it going out, or "going out" (with a different inflection), or going steady, or hanging out, or courting, or just friends? Trying to keep up with the current terminology is a real challenge. Difficult issues and no easy answers. But here are some guidelines.

Discuss Dating Before It Happens

Talk about dating when your child is young. Use TV shows, news, headlines, and weddings to talk about dating and marriage. Help your kids see that dating isn't an isolated event. It's learning how to build a friendship that could lead to marriage. Emphasize the importance of marrying a believer (2 Cor. 6:14). This is a nonnegotiable. But you need to explain *why*. What difference would it make? Ultimately it will be your child's choice, not yours.

What about dating nonbelievers? This is an issue on which believers will disagree. There is not a right answer. Your position will depend on your relationship with your teen and the circumstances of the event. Suppose a neighborhood boy asks your daughter to homecoming. His parents are good friends of yours. He's a good kid. However, they are not believers. The kids are *just* friends. It's a convenient date for an important function. Are you going to say she can't go? I think we have to be very careful here not to be too legalistic. It's easy to make an issue out of something and do damage to relationships when it's not necessary. On the other hand, I would not want my teen to move from going out as a friend into a dating relationship with a nonbeliever. Once you begin to cross "the line" from friend to date, you are headed for pain. Be alert to "the line" and stay in close communication with your child.

There is not one magic age when a child is ready to go out as friends or to date. Kids are so different. But in general, going out as a single couple before age sixteen is risky. It is not going to hurt our kids to wait. Remember the importance of learning to wait. Double-dating is the best way to begin to date.

Know the Date

You must be the most involved when your kids first start to date. Be sure you get to know your child's date. You may have to cancel your own plans to be available. Do research to find out all you can about the potential date. Be especially wary if there is a big age difference. Talk to other parents and teachers. As your kids gain experience, you will need to loosen up and be less involved. But always get to know your child's date. It's a way of being interested in him and his friends.

Blind dates, unless set up by a trustworthy friend who knows the person well, are out. There's too much risk in today's world.

Have Curfews

Curfews. The dreaded word. Why have them? For protection. Not much good happens after midnight.

Set a specific time to be in. Younger teens have earlier curfews. As they get older, we loosen up. For certain special events we negotiate the curfew. When you establish curfews and stick to them, kids will learn it's family policy, and the arguments will lessen.

But how do we know if they come in on time?

You may have to stay up to greet them and to hear about their date. You will be exhausted, but it's a brief season, and some of the best talks with teens happen late at night.

One mom set the alarm in her bedroom to ring at curfew time. If her child came in and turned it off, she knew he was home. Another mom went to sleep in her daughter's bed. She definitely knew when her teen came in!

What if *his* date doesn't have a curfew?

This happened to us. It's embarrassing for him when *he* has to be in and *she* doesn't. I simply said to my son, "Just tell her you have the strictest parents in town." And we laughed. He didn't think it was all that funny, but he knew there was no sense arguing; it was family policy.

Our kids had curfews all the way through high school. In their later years we negotiated the curfew depending upon the event. Today when they come home from college, I ask them to tell me what time they will be in, and they do. It's being considerate of us, their parents.

Establish Clear Family Policies

If you call it *policy* and not *rules* it will go over better. Here are some of ours:

- *We always know where our kids are, what time they will be in,* and *whom they are with. If any of the above plans change, they call.* We parents are bound by this same policy. It's considerate. Our kids need to know where we are in case they need us.

- *Our kids don't go to someone's house where there is not an adult present.* In an era when many parents work away from home, houses are often empty after school. It is important for a stay-at-home parent to open her house for teens.

- *Our kids don't entertain the opposite sex at our home if an adult is not present.* Empty houses simply aren't safe. We have a little farm an hour out of town. It's always been family policy, even for our college kids, that you don't go to the farm with a date unchaperoned. It's walking into temptation. God's Word tells us in many places to flee the temptation of immorality, not flirt with it. (See 1 Cor. 6:18; 10:14; 2 Tim. 2:22.)

- *Bedrooms are off-limits for the opposite sex.* Give the kids some other space in your home and stay out of their way. We'll talk more about this in the next chapter.

- *We don't leave our kids at home alone to go out of town.* Even if they are trustworthy. Our friends did this, and word got out among the teenagers. A crowd from a nearby school came over, pushed their way into the home, and trashed the house while partying. Finally, the son was able to get some help. Their kids were trustworthy. Others were not.

- *We are not afraid to say no.* A tradition in the South is a week at the beach after high school exams are over. Guys and girls all go together. It's "the thing to do" in some areas. Usually it's just one long drunken week with unchecked passion. It's best to say early in the teen years, before the request is made, "Kids, we want you to know now that we don't do beach week in our family. It's not safe. It can put you in a dangerous environment that you can't control. We felt it would be most fair to let you know this ahead of time."

You might discuss other options with your kids for events like beach week, like going yourself and renting a house at the beach in which your kids and a few friends can stay with you, or planning an in-town party. You will not be popular for your stand, but your kids will be safe.

Say no to coed slumber parties. In an attempt to keep kids off the road or keep them where parents are, coed slumber parties are cropping up—teens staying together in one house after a late-night activity, supposedly sleeping in different areas with good intentions. But it is not wise. It promotes what I call *false bonding*. Brushing your teeth together is something you do when you're married. Putting our kids in a situation in which they are artificially close encourages a false intimacy. It makes them feel closer than they actually are.

A different aspect of false bonding can happen on family vacations. Think long and hard before you invite a boyfriend or girlfriend on a family vacation or to a family wedding. A family vacation is just that—family. Having dates along can make them feel like family when they are not. This is false bonding and pushes our high school teen's relationship with someone to a level for which it is not yet ready. This makes breaking up even more difficult.

As you implement your family policies, take the time to discuss with your child the *whys* behind the policies. Simply laying out rules will only backfire. You are giving your child parameters to protect him, but you are also training him to make wise decisions. He needs to know *why* you make your decisions, even if he doesn't like them. Ask for his input on policies, and incorporate whatever you can. This demonstrates that you value his growing maturity. But remember that the family is not a democracy. You are still the parent.

Drinking and Drugs

Recently I was speaking in a church to parents of teens. During the question-and-answer time, one parent asked, "How can we teach our kids to drink responsibly?"

Pausing for courage, I simply said, "Responsible drinking for teenagers is an oxymoron. We cannot teach our teens to drink responsibly. Drinking under the age of twenty-one is against the law in all fifty states."

Laws are crafted for our protection, and as believers we should be the first to obey the law of the land unless it contradicts the law of God.

Therefore, our family policy is no drinking under age twenty-one. When we begin to talk about this in the early teen years, they will be more likely to go off to college with the commitment not to drink. Making this drinking policy a family nonnegotiable will eliminate many problems.

A recent study conducted by the National Institutes of Health concluded that one in four children is exposed to familial alcohol abuse before age eighteen.[8]

You may need to ask some hard questions: Is drinking a problem for you? How much liquor do you have in your home? You will have to be open to your teen challenging you on your behavior, and you will have to be willing to take needed steps to change your habits if your teen requests this. If parents differ in their views, there will likely be tension. We cannot control our spouse's behavior, but we can talk to our teen about the dangers of alcohol. If serious problems persist, take advantage of Alcoholics Anonymous. They have programs for spouses (Al-Anon) and teens (Al-Ateen) who live with an alcoholic parent.[9] This is not something you should try to handle alone.

So what do you do when your child wants to go to a party where alcohol will be served? They don't go. Parents are liable for serving alcohol. Police can bust the party and arrest your child. If you begin this policy in the early teen years, it is less likely to become a hot issue.

But what about seniors in high school? After all, they are about to go to college, where they can do whatever they want. Should we loosen up?

Perhaps your child, a senior, doesn't drink but goes along as the designated driver. Depending upon your relationship with your child and his lifestyle, this might be right for you. But be sure you both understand that in some states he is liable if a party is raided, even if he isn't drinking himself.

Our believing kids need to learn the principle of avoiding the appearance of evil. God's Word is clear on this matter. We are not to do anything that might cause another to stumble (1 Cor. 8:9). If our twelfth-grade teen goes to Bible study on Wednesday but is at the drinking party on Friday, what message does this send to the tenth-grade guys he's trying to influence?

What about Smoking?

A study just conducted by the Centers for Disease Control has found that one in eight students in grades six through nine is using tobacco.[10] What's alarming about this study is the young ages at which kids are smoking and the variety of products from which they can choose (cigarettes, cigars, bidis, kreteks, to name a few). Smoking is addictive and unhealthy at the least. It can lead to smoking pot and to involvement in other drugs.

So what do we do? Our response depends upon the age of our child, what is going on in his life, and our relationship with him. For a middle schooler this is a *crucial issue*. It should not be permitted. Our child is far too young to appreciate the long-term consequences of his actions. If, on the other hand, you are dealing with a rebellious eighteen-year-old, we may have to let this be a *swing issue*. As our kids get older, we have to loosen up and pick our battles carefully. We may not like the smoking, but we may be dealing with more significant issues with this child, and thus we have to choose to let this one go.

What about Drugs?

Part of being a teenager involves self-discovery, a search for personal meaning. Eugene Peterson says, "Drug use at least in its early stages feels spiritual—there is a sense of getting to the heart of things, of transcending the petty and mundane irritations of ordinary life, of entering something large and beautiful and peaceful."[11]

It's helpful to understand this in order to establish a rapport with your teen. Talk with your kids about drugs in the elementary years. Continue having conversations in the middle school years. Conversation is two-way, not merely our "preaching." Ask them about drug use they've noticed, what they think about drugs. Listen to them. If you stay involved in your child's life, you will be more likely to notice unusual behavior that could signal drug use. If you sense your child is experimenting with drugs, you must confront the issue in love. And you *must* get help. A parent cannot handle this alone. Drug abuse is a serious, life-threatening issue, and it requires expert help. It's important to get treatment first and then work through understanding.

Grades

"But I *have* studied. You're always on my back!"

No matter how hard we try or what we do, we will still hear this statement. It just goes with this season. Part of our job description *is* to nag. No, we don't like it, and neither do they, but we can't completely alleviate it either. However, several things will help us nag less and encourage more as we deal with the tension of grades.

Establish Clear Family Policies in the Area of Studies

Knowing what is expected will enable us to nag less because our kids will learn, "It's just the way it is at our house."

Our policy should serve to support our teen as he strives to do his best. Yates' policy says we don't go out on school nights unless there's a specific reason (ball game, study session).

Sally couldn't figure out why her daughter was barely passing in school.

"What does she do on school nights?" I asked.

"Oh, I don't know; she's always out," was Sally's response.

Yates' policy says we don't watch TV or videos on school nights after the early evening news. (Occasional exceptions are permitted, like during the NCAA basketball tourney.)

"But what if I've finished all my homework?"

"That's great! Now you have time to read a book."

Our kids are losing the art and joy of reading. Reading develops vocabulary. Verbal SAT scores are directly related to vocabulary. We desperately need to encourage our kids to read, not merely for good test scores but also for their own pleasure.

What about the computer? Isn't it educational? Yes, but it's also a source of chat rooms, pornography, and games. And it keeps kids from reading. Have a family policy that sets limits on computer time, and be sure you know what your child is doing on the computer.

How much help do we give our kids with their homework? Give them more in the early years and then steadily pull back. Once your teen reaches high school, he should not need much assistance. If he requests help, advise him—but do not write his papers. Not only is this dishonest, it's also overparenting. If you have several kids, you can establish a homework helping order. The eldest helps the next, who helps the next, and so forth. This can relieve an exhausted parent and aid in building sibling relationships.

Encourage your child as he studies. Write him notes saying you are proud of him. Provide snacks; help him pick a good place to study. Let him determine if he listens to music or not while studying. You may need to limit phone calls, but it's best to negotiate a phone policy with your child.

When you make clear policies with the first child and follow through with them, it will make it easier with subsequent children because they will know this is "just how we do it."

Remember, Each Child Is Different

No two children are alike. One may need more structure than another. One may excel in math and science, while his sibling struggles in this area. Your child may be very different from you. A wise parent will not compare his children to each other. "Why can't you be more like . . ." is a deadly phrase. It only makes our child feel "less than."

Driving

Getting a driver's license calls for a celebration! Go out for a treat. Have a special family meal. Create a party. It's a milestone in a child's life, and we want to take every opportunity we can to celebrate with our teens.

But while the license represents *freedom* to our child, it represents *fear* to us. After all, we know that the car can be a dangerous weapon. It's not just our child that causes us to fear, it's the other drivers on the road.

Our teens tend to think of driving as a *right*; we have to help them understand it's a *privilege and a responsibility*.

Our friends Rich and Sue developed a contract they had their son Richie sign before he got his license. I think it's such a good idea, I've included it here:

Driving Contract

Richie promises to Mom and Dad the following:

I will obey all speed limits.

I will not eat any food or consume any drinks while driving.

I will not play music loudly.

I will keep two hands on the wheel.

I will not have any passengers in the car until December 1 (except for Peter and Emily [his siblings]). But all arrangements to carry passengers afterward need to be approved in advance by Mom and Dad.

If I receive a ticket, I will pay for it out of my own money.

I will only drive the car with permission from Mom or Dad. I will tell them where I am going and when I will be home. If I want to change my plans, I will call to get permission before I go anywhere.

I will not use the telephone while driving. If the phone rings, I will pull over to answer it. If I need to make a call, I will pull over.

Everyone in the car will wear seat belts or the car doesn't move. There can never be more passengers than seat belts.

I may not drive on Interstate 495, I-66, the Dulles Toll Road, or any other interstate without permission.

This contract can be changed to add or remove terms at any time if we agree.

We are proud of your progress and the sense of responsibility you have been showing.

October 29

Mom's signature _____

Dad's signature _____

Richie's signature _____

Notice that these wise parents were clear with their expectations. They discussed the whys of every point with their son. And notice that there was a period of a month before Richie was allowed to drive anyone but his family. This gave him time to build up his driving skills. I encourage you to use this as a sample and prepare one for you and your child.

Money

One of the greatest sources of marital conflict is money. The Scriptures say that the love of money is a root of all kinds of evil (1 Tim. 6:10). Either we have too much, love it, and are miserably empty, or we don't have enough, want more, and are miserable. We must teach our kids to handle money at a young age. We are not only training them to be good stewards, we are training them for marriage. Everything we have is a gift from God. We are to be good stewards of His gifts. Here are a few tips for helping your teen grow in this area.

Train Them to Give, Save, and Work

Malachi 3:10 encourages us to tithe. A tithe means giving the first 10 percent to the Lord. Ten percent should not be the goal but the starting place from which we can increase our giving. Encourage your teen to open a separate checking account or have a separate envelope for his tithe. He should put 10 percent of everything he earns into this account. He will get pleasure being the one to decide where his tithe should go. A different account or envelope should be used for savings. A minimum of 10 percent should go into this account. For some, investing a portion of savings in the stock market can be a great learning experience.

Our kids need to learn the value of work. Even if you can supply their financial needs, don't give them everything. Be careful with overdoing allowances. How you handle allowances should be determined by your principles, not by what your friend's children get. Encourage your kids to pursue moneymaking opportunities. Not only are you teaching them the value of work, you are increasing their own self-confidence.

Teach Them to Budget

By the time they reach tenth grade, teens should have a checking account. They should be responsible for balancing it. They should draw up their own monthly budget. Be very clear about what you pay for and what they pay for. You'll have to help them initially, but then turn it over to them and simply check in to see how it's going. It may seem silly to teach them to budget when they have so little, but you are teaching a principle. They must learn to be faithful in small things in order to be able to handle big things (Matt. 25:23; Luke 16:10). Celebrate their first checking account. Tell them how proud you are that they are growing in the area of handling their finances.

We put our twins on a clothing allowance in high school. They were given a certain amount from us to buy their basic clothes. We were specific about what they covered and what we covered outside the allowance. When Libby "just had to have" a certain bathing suit, I warned her that it would deplete her clothing allowance. But she insisted and bought the suit. Later she had no money to buy a skirt she really needed. I didn't say, "I told you so," even though I wanted to! I simply said, "I'm so sorry." Everything in me wanted to bail her out, to give her the money. But I knew I couldn't. She had to learn. I had to be willing to be embarrassed when she wore her old skirt. My embarrassment was not nearly as important as the lesson she learned in budgeting.

Insist They Operate Debt-Free

If your child has a credit card, limit it to only one, primarily to be used in emergencies. It's better for them to operate on a cash basis. A credit card must be paid off *in full* each month. I learned this the hard way. Susy and I were shopping. She wanted a CD, which she was going to put on her credit card. I asked her, "Do you already have the money in cash to be able to pay off your credit card if you charge this?"

"No," she responded. "I'll worry about it later."

"Honey," I replied, "I'm sorry, but I cannot let you buy a CD. I want to in the worst way, but part of my job as a parent is to teach you how to handle money. The hardest lesson to learn is that you cannot spend what you do not have. You cannot buy anything until you pay the bill for what you already owe."

She was not happy. I was not happy either, but both of us learned an important lesson.

It's important to learn to live debt-free, and this includes borrowing from parents, friends, or siblings. (Bank loans for home mortgages and perhaps autos may be an exception, but that's *way* in their future!) For our teens, the rule of thumb should be, "If the money cannot be paid back today, don't borrow."

Encourage Them to Be Creative

Homecomings and proms can mean fancy dresses, expensive dinners, and limos. But these events don't have to be pricey to be fun. Once our son John and two of his friends decided that instead of taking their dates to an expensive restaurant, they would do the shopping and cook an elegant dinner for them at our house. They closed off the dining room, put on their favorite music, used the best china, lit lots of candles, and hired the twins to act as waitresses and dishwashers. Dressed in "approved" costume, the twins greeted the guests at the front door, saying, "Welcome to Chez Garçon." Their dates were very impressed!

Remember Parental Peer Pressure

It's easy to fall prey to parental peer pressure in the area of finances. We want our teen to dress like our friends' kids, to go places their kids do, to have what their teens have. After all, we want our child to feel good about herself. In reality, we want to make sure *we look good as a parent*. It's important to ask myself, *What principle am I communicating?*

Amy and Marian have become good friends through the youth ministry at their church. Amy lives in a tiny three-bedroom apartment with her mom and four siblings. She has an after-school job to earn her spending money. Their family does not take vacations. Just having enough money for the weekly grocery bill is their goal. Marian, on the other hand, lives in a large home in a fashionable neighborhood. She takes wonderful trips with her parents, and they own a second home. The friendship of these two girls has enriched both families. They have learned that things or lack of things doesn't matter nearly as much as the friendship.

Having friends in different economic situations will help to alleviate some of this intense pressure. It will also be much healthier for you personally and for your kids.

Learn to Be Content in All Situations

Above all, we desire to teach our teens to be content in all situations and to hold their possessions with an open fist, free to give away or to let go, rather than with a clenched fist. Teenagers are more overwhelmed with comparison than with contentment. We must appreciate this tension in their lives but also ask ourselves some tough questions.

What is the subject of conversation in our family? Do we speak often of who is wealthy, how much money so-and-so has, whose house is the biggest? If we do, our children will learn that money is most important. Do we complain because we can't afford something or because we don't have the funds to do such and such? If we do, our children will grow up with ungrateful hearts. Do we criticize those with more, and do we put down those with less? If we do, we are nurturing a critical spirit. In each case we are unconsciously promoting comparison rather than contentment.

The apostle Paul says, "For I have learned to be content whatever the circumstances" (Phil. 4:11). This is a good prayer for ourselves and for our kids.

Media

TV, movies, videos, music, and the Internet. Help! There are too many choices, too many options, and it's so hard to discern what's good, what's bad, what's too much.

Space doesn't permit an in-depth analysis, so consider this a starting place for doing your own research to establish your own family policies. As you do this, keep in mind that it is best to be the firmest in these areas when you have young teens and then gradually loosen up as they move through high school.

Television

"I can't get him to turn it off!"

Why? Who is the parent? Simply turn it off, unplug it, or have it taken out. Yes, he'll pitch a fit. But you don't have to get into a huge argument; simply turn it off. If you've already established school night guidelines, you won't have as many battles.

Watch what your children watch. Ask, "What values does this show promote?" Discuss the show with them.

One dad watched a favorite TV show with his son with the following agreement: "I'll give you a quarter every time you point out a value being promoted that is not a moral value." His son got a lot of quarters, but more importantly, he learned to evaluate and question what he was viewing instead of accepting it.

Thirty-minute TV shows leave you with the assumption that problems can be solved quickly. Lives are changed and problems solved in one episode. A steady dose of this will instill in our kids an unrealistic expectation of instant solutions to life's problems.

Don't permit your children to have TVs in their rooms. It's unnecessary, and it only heightens the issue. A TV in a family room is enough.

Movies and Videos

We always had the policy that you don't go to a movie or rent a video that's rated anything other than PG unless we have seen it or another adult has who has the same standards that we do. We make adjustments as our kids reach their senior year. There is rarely any reason to see an R-rated movie. Johnny and the boys saw *Schindler's List* (rated R) together. That was an exception. Keep in mind that we are impacted by what we see. There is a big difference between reading a description of a World War II battle and watching the graphic violence on the screen. Some men and women are more impacted by what they see. It's very difficult to remove the visual images. If your teen is visually sensitive, he should not see a movie that his sibling might. Do not make him feel "less than." He is gifted, and he is wise in choosing not to watch the film. Be very careful in what you permit your teens to go see or to bring home to watch. And guard what you yourself watch. The apostle Paul reminds us, "Do not conform any longer to the pattern of this world, but be transformed by the renewing of your mind" (Rom. 12:2).

Ask, "How will this show impact the renewing of my mind?"

We don't want to be all negative. More and more good films are being produced! Many of these our teens will like, and many will be fun for families to watch together. Gateway Films Vision Video is an excellent resource.[12]

The Internet

The Internet has changed our world, and it's only just begun. Much of it is good, and much of it is bad. The easy access of pornography is a grave danger to our teens, particularly our sons. It is rampant in the Christian community because it is a "secret sin." It is addictive. Talk openly with your children about pornography. Discuss the attraction, the dangers. Be clear in your family policy. No pornography of any kind ever for anyone, adults included. This is always a crucial issue. If this is a problem for you, the parent, get help (see Resource section).

Know what your children are doing on the computer. One mom discovered that her son had looked at some pornography on their computer. She moved the computer into her bedroom, and her son had to go there to use it. She learned how to put certain blocks on some sites, and she learned how to check what had been viewed. This can be difficult, because our kids usually know more about using the computer than we do. Get a computer-savvy friend to help you with this. It's crucial to have clear communication with your teen and to talk openly about this issue.

Too much time spent on the computer can have other consequences. It retards social interaction. Our teens don't learn how to talk and how to interact with people. We are in danger of raising a generation of kids who do not know how to relate to people. Too much TV and video watching has the same impact. Often teens want to have friends over and rent a movie. Discourage this. They will not learn how to talk with one another. Instead have food, games, sports, and a plan. Let "movie night" be a rare exception rather than a weekly event.

Music

Do we let our kids listen to secular music? Or do we insist they listen only to Christian music? How do we know what music is good and what is bad? How can we understand the words? Balance is needed here. Some secular music is good, and some Christian music is lousy. A musically gifted teen may listen to a secular tape that sounds terrible to us. It's too loud and too noisy. We hear the noise; he hears the different beats. Listen to the music with your teen. What do the lyrics say? Why does he like this music? Ask him, "How do these words make you feel? What do you think the message is? Do you agree? Why or why not?"

If your teen is being drawn into a music subculture that you believe is dangerous, you must take action. You are the parent. How you deal with this potentially hot topic will depend upon the relationship you have with your child.

Do whatever you can to expose your teens to good Christian music. Take them to concerts by popular Christian bands. Give them CDs by Christian artists. Encourage them to spend time with an older friend who is solid in his faith and loves music. An older mentor can help your teen learn to distinguish between good and evil and to evaluate what music is appropriate. Your teen is more likely to heed his words than yours.

In handling each of these hot topics, be sensitive to the other issues that you are dealing with in your relationship with your teen. You may have to let something be a swing issue in order to focus on a more crucial issue at this particular time. Keep communication channels open. Take the time to learn everything you can about your child's world and his personal interests. You may have to set aside your own interests in order to have time to do this, but it is a brief season, and how you relate over the hot topics will be influenced by your involvement in his life in other areas.

Focus Questions

Meditate on Proverbs 1. We need wisdom to handle hot topics! What do you learn about wisdom from this chapter?

1. Which hot topic is an issue in your family right now? Is there specific teaching in the Scriptures on this topic? What steps can you take to lessen the "sizzle" of this hot issue? (For example: agree as parents on the issue, clarify your policy, communicate the *whys* of your policy to your teen.)
2. List other hot topics that have occurred or will be likely to occur in your family. What will your family policy be on each topic? Write down your current thoughts. Keep in mind that you will need to refine and update your approach.

3. It is very helpful to have a few other parents with whom you agree on policy. These should be parents with children approximately the ages of yours. Design a "Parent's Policy" on whatever issues you can and determine to stick together on implementation. This will give you support and give your teens a sense that their parents "aren't the only ones who . . ." They may not like it, but it will give them a sense of security.

Meditate further on the Book of Proverbs. Read one chapter each day, matching the day of the month to the proverb (there are 31 chapters).

The fear of the LORD is the beginning of knowledge
but fools despise wisdom and discipline.

Proverbs 1:7

7

Taking Advantage of Peer Pressure

But all my friends get to . . .

My husband and I were speaking at a family conference in the Northwest. Scores of families with children of all ages had gathered together for a week of talks, sports, music, and good old fun. Many of the families had preteens and teens. Those parents with preteens were especially interested in discussing the teen years. One evening we put together a panel of teenagers to help us adults glean some perspective into their world.

"If there was one piece of advice you would give to parents as their kids approach the teen years, what would it be?" we asked the kids.

"Stop talking about the teen years being awful. You give us a negative reputation that we haven't earned before we even get there. If you will talk about the teen years as positive years, we will be more likely to live up to that reputation," they replied.

Peer pressure, teen rebellion, teen power. All strike fear and dread in a parent. But do these years with so many "hot issues" have to be awful? Is peer pressure always negative? Does this season have to have an "us" (parents) versus "them" (teens) mentality?

It doesn't. Peer pressure is important. It can be difficult. But it doesn't necessarily have to be negative. If we understand what is happening to our teens and approach the peer influence issue with care, we can turn this into a positive time of interaction.

"My daughter is pulling away from me. She doesn't tell me the things she used to. She's closing me out. She's so into her friends. What they think is more important than what I say. She spends all her time on the phone with her door shut."

"I'm worried about my son; I don't really like the guys he's hanging out with. He'd rather be with them than with the family. He insists on wearing jeans that are way too big and look like they are going to fall off any second. He's starting to look and act like someone I don't know."

"I feel like I don't know what's going on, and it's scary. Their friends have more power than I do."

"I'm losing control."

What is going on? Does this sound like your home? If so, be encouraged. It's normal.

For the time being, friends seem to have superseded parents as the most important influence in our child's life. Friends dictate what's in, what's out, who's popular, who's not.

Yes, we may know better than their friends. However, we must accept the stress they are under and the conflict they feel. How our kids respond to peers is going to vary widely. Some will be supersensitive to "the crowd," while others will not care that much. One of your children may be a natural leader, while another is more of a follower. A thirteen-year-old boy and a nineteen-year-old girl will be miles apart in how they relate to peers.

In this season, we have the opportunity to adopt a "you and yours" mentality instead of an "us versus them" mentality. It's the attitude that says, "Hey, I like who you are becoming. I understand how important your friends are to you, and I want to know your friends." This will pave the way for shared, intergenerational friendships as your children approach the late teens and early twenties.

There are six gifts we can give our children that will help us harness peer pressure in a positive way. Not one of these gifts has any monetary value. Yet each gift will be costly in terms of your time and convenience. However, you will never regret the investment.

Gift One: Make Your Home the Hangout

The most important purchase I made during the teen years cost ten dollars. I got it at a garage sale. It's ugly, and it takes up room that could be used for something else. It's a source of noise and confusion, frustration and delight. And it keeps me up late at night. It's a Ping-Pong table.

With five teenagers, I quickly learned that it is important to do whatever you can to make your home the hangout. Our Ping-Pong table is in the garage. There's no other place to put it. In the summer the garage door stays open, and the kids use the garage as their recreation room. In the winter they play in their coats.

A Ping-Pong table attracts kids, but so does food. If you have it, they will come! A big item in our budget is food.

My friend Vicky is a great cook. Her specialty is sourdough bread. Recently she said to her seventeen-year-old daughter, "If you'll bring the gang over after school, I'll have hot bread waiting." They came.

Why do we want our home to be the teen center? We can control what goes on in our home. We cannot control what goes on in someone else's home. And having the kids at our place provides us with a natural opportunity to get to know our kids' friends. In the process, we will get to know our own child better as we watch him interact with his peers.

As you make your home a hangout, the following will be helpful.

Do be willing to postpone your own social life. You will often have to say no to going out with your friends in order to stay home on the weekend so your kids can have their friends over. It will be hard, but it's only for a brief season, and it's worth it.

Do hold off on redecorating. Your couch may be gross, the carpet in need of replacing, the walls gray with handprints, but it's better to wait. You want to create a friendly, comfortable atmosphere, not one that communicates, "Don't get mud on the new couch; don't touch the walls; wipe your feet before you track on the carpet."

Do have curfews. It's family policy. Simply say to your kids ahead of time, "The house closes tonight at midnight" (or whatever time you set with your teen—but be specific). "Anyone who doesn't live here needs to go, and everyone who lives here needs to stay in!"

Do have expectations. Your kids should clean up. If your kids understand this, they will learn to get their friends to help so that they aren't stuck with it all by themselves. This is a character issue. It has to do with thoughtfulness. You don't want to face a huge mess in the morning. Yes, special events will call for grace in this area (cleaning up the next day), but generally, expect the teens to have cleaned up. Remember, you are training future husbands and wives. Thoughtfulness is crucial in marriage.

Do be a presence. It may feel awkward. Do I hang around or get out of their way? It's a little of both. The age of the teens and whether it's both sexes will help determine how much you hang out. It's most comfortable if you are present at the beginning of the gathering and at the end.

Do try to talk to each guest. You are modeling good manners. Before the gathering, get your teen to tell you who is coming. Ask him for things to talk about with specific friends. "Son, I don't know Thad very well. What is he into? What can I talk with him about?" Ask your teen how you can help her friends feel comfortable.

Do have an "open door, lights on" policy. Dark basement family rooms with lights out and doors shut can be an invitation to temptation, especially with opposite sexes. Simply tell your kids this is family policy. It's for protection. It's not a matter of trust. It's a matter of wisdom. Wise people don't put themselves into tempting situations. It's your house.

Do stay up, at least one parent. It's not wise to turn a home over to young teens and go to bed. You are still the hosts. Do give them some space and go to another room. You will be tired. But it's a short season.

Does my home always have to be the hangout home? It's summer; they are up every night at our house. I'm exhausted. I have to get up and go to work. It's time to call a break.

"Hey, Son, you know I love having your friends over, but we're exhausted and we need a break. You also need a break. You don't have to do something every night. Let's designate tomorrow night (or this weekend) as family time and stay home without company."

Gift Two: Spend Time in Their World

When our son John was a high school junior, I went on his student government leadership retreat. I was a parent chaperone and stayed in a room with some of the teachers. Our walls were thin, and we could hear everything in the student girls' room next to us. Obscene language, who was doing what sexually with whom, which teachers "sucked." It was simultaneously embarrassing, horrifying, and enlightening. It gave me a window into my son's world. And it gave me empathy for those teachers!

Walk the halls of your child's school. Offer to drive car pools to sporting events and performances. As I've mentioned earlier, the car is a tremendous research lab.

When you go to your child's events, don't take your laptop and sit in the back. What this communicates is, "I'm just trying to get credit for being here, I'm not really paying attention to what is going on, and I have more important things to do."

My son's friend Nate grew up in a single-parent home. His mom made many sacrifices to be supportive of him.

When I asked him to share with me an impact she had had on his life, he responded, "Even though Mom had to get up early to get to work, she still came to my ball games. I remember one particular game for which she drove two hours in rush-hour traffic. It was a game that didn't even matter in rankings. Only three other parents bothered to show up. But she was there. Her presence at my games gave me a sense of security, confidence, and comfort. Her presence has given me a better understanding of God's presence. I know that He will always be there for me even when she is no longer able to be."

Gift Three: Get to Know Their Friends

My son John said to me, "Mom, it's important for Justin to come over to our house. He doesn't get a lot of encouragement from his parents. He's an artist, and they don't understand him. Will you ask him to bring by some of his pictures to show you?"

I realized my son was telling me more than was obvious. He was telling me, "Spend time with my friends. Be interested in them. Ask them questions. Draw them out. Cheer for them."

Sometimes we don't know how to talk to teens. I have found it helpful to think in terms of schedules and relationships. Everyone has schedules, and everyone has relationships. Brainstorm questions that fall into these two categories. What's your hardest class this semester? (schedule question). Who do you like to hang out with on weekends? (relationship question). If we ask, "How was your day?" we are likely to hear, "Fine." Period. But if we learn to ask questions that call for more than a one-word answer, we'll get to know our children and their friends.

Have fun with your teen's friends. Two of the twins' friends, Sarah and Susie, came to visit us at the beach. After several fun days together, they had to leave. Early in the morning, I slipped out to Susie's car and hid a dead, smelly crab in it. You can imagine their shock when they opened the door to the car, which had been sitting in the summer heat. We roared with laughter. But the "war" had just begun. Weeks later these two gals were over at our house. When Johnny and I went to bed that night, our bed was not only short-sheeted but was heavily sprinkled with Old Bay crab seasoning! Ah, retribution!

What If I Don't Like My Child's Friends?

If my child has friends that I don't like, how should I handle this situation? Very carefully. Teens are fickle, but they are also very loyal when it comes to their friends and you. To help discern the wisest response, consider several questions.

What is my child's age? Young teens, especially girls, switch friends often. It may be prudent to stay quiet and pray this particular friendship passes.

What is my child's personality? For example, at this stage in life, is my child a chameleon? A chameleon takes on the color of his surroundings in order to blend in. Does my teen take on the personality and values of whomever she's with? Is she overly dependent on friends? A follow-up question would be, Is my child a follower or a leader, the one influencing or the one being influenced? Your child's age, personality, maturity, and relationship with you will determine how you handle this tough relationship. There is not one pat answer.

But how do I know if I should intervene? We have to guard against overreacting. Part of letting go means letting them choose their own friends. Yes, they will make some mistakes. But often after a period of time the relationship will end on its own.

Ask yourself, Is this relationship impacting other areas of his life? Other friendships? His studies? Sibling relationships? Our relationship? Eating habits? Sleeping habits? Is it a possessive relationship? Talk to a teacher, to other parents who know your child, and to his youth minister to see what they are observing.

Talk to your child. Pick a neutral time. Ask, "Son, tell me what you admire in this friend?" Be prepared to do lots of listening. Be honest about your concerns without being too critical of the friend. "I'm concerned about. . . . I sense he has a good heart but is. . . . I'm concerned that. . . ."

If after assessing, listening, observing, gathering information, and praying, you sense danger, then you have to take action. You are the parent.

It's easier to take action if your child is a young teen. Work behind the scenes. Put your child into activities in which the friend is not involved. Request different classes in school. Encourage get-togethers with other potential friends. If your child is an older teen, it will be more difficult, because you have to let go more.

Honesty is always the best policy. Get advice from a wise, believing adult. Agree as a couple on the action to be taken. If you are a single parent, devise an action plan with another couple. Get a friend to pray for your conversation with your child. Say, "Son, your mother and I do not feel that your relationship with Don is a healthy one. This is why . . ." (Be specific.) "I know this is terribly painful for you; he's your friend. We don't like this either, but you are our child, and we love you. As parents we have to do what we think is best for you. Therefore we don't want you to spend time with him." (Be specific as to what your expectations are: At all? Except at our house? Only when?) "This is not necessarily forever, Son. We promise to pray regularly for your friend and his family."

Ask your child if he would like you to help him think of how or if he should communicate this to the friend. He may not want your help. That's okay. If the unhealthy relationship is between opposite sexes, you may need to take action sooner rather than later.

In extreme situations, don't be afraid to take drastic steps. Friends of ours pulled their daughter out of a certain school and sent her to a different one because of the crowd she was involved in. Even though the school had been good for her siblings, her wise parents realized this particular child, drawn to potentially harmful friendships, was in over her head and needed a lifeboat. It was not an easy choice. It was inconvenient, and everyone had to make sacrifices. But it was the right choice, and now, two years later, with confidence and maturity under her belt, she's ready for her final years back in the neighborhood school.

What If My Teen Doesn't Have Any Friends?

Some of us need lots of friends, and others gravitate to one or two. We are each different. It's important not to project our own relationship needs onto our children. She may be fine with one close friend; he may exhaust us with the gang he runs with.

If your teen doesn't seem to have a friend, pray for God to bring one into his life. Be proactive. Ask a teacher for guidance in who might be a good friend for your son. Teachers can be a big help. They see our kids in ways that we don't. Plan an event that will appeal to your teen. Get an extra ticket somewhere for him to bring a friend. It's a lot easier for a shy teen to invite a friend along to an activity like a concert or sports event where success is almost guaranteed than to simply have a potential friend over to hang out.

Teens need to develop same-sex friendships. Be alert to a daughter who seems to gravitate to serious relationships with boys yet doesn't have any close girlfriends. This is unhealthy. In order to have healthy relationships with the opposite sex, we need to learn how to develop deep friendships with the same sex. Girls need girlfriends; boys need boyfriends.

Gift Four: Get to Know the Other Parents

My son's friend was planning a boy-girl party at her house. They were going to turn the lights down low and dance. It made me uncomfortable because these kids were just in seventh grade. I knew this family did not have the same values that we did. But I didn't know what to do. My son was exasperated. "Everyone else is going, Mom; it's okay," he urged.

"I can't give you an answer right now, Son. I have to think about this," I replied.

I didn't really know this mom, but I did know she and her family were not people of faith. I didn't want to come across as paranoid. I longed to be able to reason with her in a manner that she would understand. I determined to approach her as if we were on the same page.

Phoning her, I said, "I wanted to talk to you about the party the kids have planned at your house. I thought it might be a good idea for us parents to put our heads together as we move into these teen years. I really appreciate your being willing to host the kids. I've been thinking, though, if we let them start this boy-girl stuff now, what will be left for them to do when they are in high school? What do you think?"

As we discussed the ramifications, she decided that they were too young to begin this and that a group of us should just say no to this at their age. Whew! I learned a good lesson. Other parents might not have thought through the requests their teens made. We can approach them without using Christian clichés. We won't always get positive results like this, but it's worth a try.

My friend Kate got a call from another seventh-grade parent.

"My daughter's coming home with all sorts of requests about what *everyone else is allowed to do*. I thought it might be good to get a bunch of parents together to talk about our kids. We're going to meet at a local restaurant for an evening next week. Spread the word to any interested parents."

Thus began a periodic gathering of parents whose kids were approximately the same age. It was especially encouraging for a single dad with a daughter. The parents didn't always agree with each other on how to handle an issue, but more importantly, they got to know one another and established relationships. Relationships that would make it easier to call one another and say, "What do you know about the kids' plans for Saturday?" A group like this can become a wonderful way to build friendships with nonbelievers.

Parents meeting together can battle the issue of "there's nothing to do." As we discuss this, remember, teens by nature are self-centered. These are the "make me happy, entertain me, and satisfy my desires" years. It's easy for us to be intimidated by their subtle threat, "Entertain me or I'll get into trouble." Boredom isn't a sin, and it's not our job to keep them busy in order to keep them out of trouble. Yes, provide fun things for them to do, but don't leave it at that. Challenge your teens to do something meaningful. Give them a vision for being a difference maker. Some of them have entrepreneurial spirits. Encourage them to think big and creatively devise ways they can make a difference in your community. As they reach out to others, they will grow in self-confidence themselves.

What If They Say, "But All My Friends Get To . . ."?

One hundred and ten seniors graduated from a prestigious private high school in Richmond, Virginia. Ninety of these graduates attended a party thrown by several of the parents. Five kegs of beer were on hand when the party was busted. Deputies administered ninety breath tests on the young party goers and determined that sixty-eight had consumed alcohol, with some breath tests ranging up to .20. (If you are above .08, you are considered legally drunk while driving.) Charges were brought against sixty-six students and nine parents. The prosecutor in the case stated that the charges related to "the underage possession of alcohol by individuals who attended the party and consumed alcohol; the adults who aided and abetted the illegal consumption of alcohol by underage attendees; and in one instance, contributing to the delinquency of minor attendees."[1]

These students were leaders in their community. Their parents were well-respected leaders and ran in elite social circles.

What of the twenty students who did not attend? Were they invited? Most likely. Did they want to go? Probably. After all, it was *the* social event of their graduation. What would you as their parent have said? What if there had been an alcohol-related accident with fatalities? Then how would the community have responded?

I'm sure the parents who hosted the party loved their kids. I'm sure they wanted to raise them right. I'm sure they were proud of them. But did they make a wise decision? No. The parents and the twenty kids who didn't attend made the wise, hard decision. Yes, those who were there but did not drink showed courage. But we have to ask: Did their mere presence condone an illegal activity? Hard questions with no easy answers.

There will be times when "everyone else gets to . . ." We have to ask, Does that make it right?

Gift Five: Encourage Other Adult Friendships

Our friend Doug has always expressed an interest in our son Chris. Doug is a visionary who dreams "outside of the box." He's unusually adept at asking good questions and interacting with teens. Chris called Doug many times for advice. Often Chris listened to Doug and followed his recommendations—the same recommendations he would not have accepted from us. Why? He was hearing it from someone other than Mom or Dad.

Other adults can play a powerful role in our teen's life. We cannot raise our kids alone. We need the body of Christ to help us. Encourage your teens to spend time with other adults who love Christ. And be willing to be that kind of adult in another child's life. It doesn't have to be a big deal.

When Chris was in public high school, he took a strong minority stand on a family-life issue at a PTA meeting. Some of the adults actually booed when they heard what he said. It was amazing. Several days later he got a letter from a parent who attended the meeting. She didn't know Chris personally. Her kids did. She wrote to tell him how proud she was of his courage in speaking out on the issues. He knew we were proud, but we're just his parents. She wasn't. He still has her letter today. A simple letter from a caring adult made a big difference in the life of a teenage boy.

Other parents and young adults will play a crucial role in your teen's faith journey. We will look at this in greater detail in the next chapter.

Gift Six: Train Them to Be a Good Friend

One of the most intense causes of pain for teens is a clique. It impacts every area of their lives. Recent high school shootings have shown us that feeling ostracized can lead to deadly violence.

It's vital that we emphasize to our kids that every person is created by God in His image. There is simply no place for snobbery. Ask your teen and some friends what they think it means to be a good friend.

Our list includes:

- Don't talk ugly about people behind their backs (don't take part in a "cut session").

- Build up one another (say one kind thing to someone today).

- Forgive one another (ask your friend to forgive you when you say or do something hurtful).

- Encourage each other to do God's will (don't cheat in school or lie to parents).

- Don't be possessive with friends (share them with others).

- Reach out to others and don't wait for them to come to you (Who in your class is lonely that you can befriend?).

Our teens will catch what is important to us. If we have close friends, they will be more likely to develop close friends. Recently I went on an overnight with my sister Fran and ten of her close friends. Every one of these women is a parent of teenagers. Each faces difficult challenges in parenting. These ten women know one another's kids. They pray for one another, weep with one another, and offer support. Their kids are blessed by this band of moms. Their kids know that someone else is keeping an eye on them. It will annoy them at times, but deep inside it gives them a sense of security.

We need different types of friends. Friends a season ahead of us who can give us perspective, friends younger than we are to keep us sharp. We need friends in different economic circumstances, friends of different races. A medley of friendships will give us a better sense of what really matters in life. We will grow in deeper ways. Our kids will be more likely to make friends with different types of people if they see us doing it.

What do we do if friends let us and our teens down?

They will, and so will we. We are all sinful people, and we will hurt each other. We have to be quick to ask forgiveness and to forgive. We have to keep short accounts, and we have to give our friends the benefit of the doubt.

We must never give up on our friends.

Allison's friend Amy had a painful home life. Her mom, a single parent, struggled to meet the needs of four teenagers. Despite the many challenges that her children presented, she remained constant in her love for them. As a sophomore, Amy began to go to youth group where she gave her life to Christ. Although she was very bright, she was a classic underachiever. Soon family struggles and unhealthy relationships weakened her academic and moral resolve, and when she graduated from high school, she became pregnant out of wedlock. Several difficult years went by, and Amy struggled as a single parent. However, during this time she came back to Christ, worked her way through college, married a wonderful believer, and is now working in full-time youth ministry.

Our God never gives up.

Focus Questions

Meditate on John 17.

1. Jesus' prayer seems to be divided into three sections. What are they? What do you learn about how Jesus cares for His friends? What does He pray for them, for others? What ideas does His example give you about praying for your teen, for your teen's friends?

2. Who are your teen's friends? What is each interested in? What is their family like? What is their favorite food? What steps can you take to get to know your teen's friends?

3. Does your child reach out to different types of people? Do you? How can you become a family that intentionally cares for the lost and lonely?

4. It is important to be an adult friend to someone else's child. What child can you befriend? How will you do this?

Meditate on Colossians 1:9–14. Make this a prayer for your teen and his or her friends.

I have made you known to them, and will continue to make you known in order that the love you have for me may be in them and that I myself may be in them. [Jesus' own prayer for your teen!]

John 17:26

8

Encouraging Your Teen's Faith

I'm not sure I believe . . .

"I don't want to go to church this morning. It's boring. I don't get anything out of it anyway. And I need my sleep. You're always saying I don't get enough sleep. Besides, I'm not sure I believe what the church says. I need to make my own decisions about God. You can't make me believe."

What is happening here? How should I respond? What if my teen rejects the faith?

Hard questions. No pat answers. Emotional turmoil for believing parents, who more than anything else long for their kids to walk with Christ.

But don't be dismayed. Part of what is happening is good. In fact, it's necessary.

What *Is* Happening?

Everyone must go through a time in which they come to the place of believing not because their parents do or their church does, but because they have determined to believe for themselves the truth of the Christian faith and have chosen to walk in this truth. It's a question of ownership. We can't live on someone else's faith or doubt the reality of faith because of someone else's lack of faith. We each have the freedom to decide for ourselves.

I was privileged to be raised in a strong Christian home. I didn't especially rebel, nor did I embrace the faith with great enthusiasm. I simply inherited it because it was part of being an Alexander. Yet there came a time in college when I was questioned about my faith by some older grad students.

One asked, "Susan, are you a Christian?"

"I think so. I hope so. I've always believed in God," I responded. He replied, "Susan, God doesn't want you to think so or hope so. He wants you to *know for sure*."

These students challenged me to accept Christ personally. They shared with me a picture of Christ standing at the door of my heart and knocking, waiting for me to open the door and invite Him into my life to be my personal Lord and Savior (Rev. 3:20). I knew that what they said had a ring of truth, and that I wanted to *know for sure* that Christ was in my life. I did ask Him into my heart. This was the turning point in my faith—a point at which I moved from an inherited faith to a personal faith. It was a necessary step for me in "owning" my faith.

The way in which each of our teens comes into a time of owning his or her faith will vary. It may be sudden and emotional, or it may be gradual and thoughtful. There is not one right way. For each of our kids (and for us) there will be many times of recommitment.

A wise parent will understand that the teen years are a time of decision in the area of faith. Is it my faith or theirs? Will they own their own faith? We won't really know the answer to this until they have left home. And it may take longer than we want.

How Should We Respond to Our Child during This Difficult Time?

We need to recognize that this time of questioning is normal. We need to do everything we can to prepare our teen to take ownership of his faith in God's time and in His way. We can pray for him, but we can't make it happen.

Only God can do that.

As we seek to encourage our teen's faith, we will have to make some adjustments. My friend Chris is a tennis pro. He teaches, and he plays in tournaments himself. Depending upon the age and the ability of the person on the other side of the net, he has to adjust his own shots. If he's teaching a beginner, his serve is soft and flat, and he hits it right to them. But if he is playing a more advanced player, he makes adjustments. He shifts his serve to more of a spin, hits it harder, and not directly to them. He knows he has to make shifts in order to bring out the best in each unique student. He has to be persistent and patient and keep at it until his student gets it. Sometimes he'll try something that doesn't work, and then he has to make further adjustments. But he doesn't give up.

In a similar way, as we raise teens we have to make two shifts in our approach to encouraging their faith. What we did with small children no longer works. Now we have to shift from predominately parental influence to utilizing positive peer pressure, and we have to shift from direct teaching to personal sharing. Let's take a look at these two shifts, beginning with utilizing peer pressure.

Shift from Parental Influence to Positive Peer Influence

A wise parent will take *advantage* of the importance of peers. Teens need peer relationships. As our kids approach their teen years, it's easy for us as parents to fear the influence of "those other kids" and to resent their power. We want to pull back as a family, to protect our child, to protect our "family's faith." This can be a mistake. Instead of withdrawing, we need to encourage our teen to pursue relationships with other kids who are seeking to follow Christ. We may have to intentionally network to help this happen. Peers are going to be pivotal in our child's spiritual journey. In fact, peers will for a time be more important to a teen than parents.

When our daughter Allison was sixteen, we sent her to a Christian conference in New England. Although we had never been, we knew the folks who ran it, and we knew it was good. Midway through her three weeks away, she called her dad.

"Dad," she exclaimed, "I've been studying this awesome book called *Knowing God* by J. I. Packer. Have you ever heard of it? [He had. In fact he'd even tried to get her to read it!] I really want you to read it so we can discuss it when I get home." What was happening here? She was hearing spiritual truth from someone other than Mom or Dad.

José's family moved to a new city his junior year in high school. Lonely, shy, and with a nationality different from most of the students, he found it hard to make friends. Everyone seemed to have their own cliques. One group, however, made an effort to include him. They invited him to parties on weekends, taught him to smoke pot, and shared their alcohol freely. Often they cruised around town "looking for beef" (kids to beat up). Even though José felt included, he was also uncomfortable with his new friends' lifestyle. Initially he was able to hide his activities from his parents, but one day his dad came home to find him drunk and sick, having thrown up all over his room. When José saw the hurt in his dad's eyes, he began to ask himself, *What's become of me?*

Even though he wasn't from a family of faith, he cried out, "God, if you are there, help me!" A few days later a girl at school invited him to a Young Life meeting. Because she was friendly, he went. There he saw kids with joy and peace, and they talked about Jesus. He had never heard about Jesus. He had only heard His name used in profanity. He didn't know about the cross or about forgiveness. A whole new world of faith and relationships opened up for José. God had heard his cry. Another student had been listening to God, and she reached out to José.

Pray for positive peers who will pursue your teen, and pray for your teen to reach out to others positively.

As we recognize the valuable role that others, especially peers, play in helping our teens come to the place of "owning their faith," the following will be helpful.

Encourage Involvement in a Vital Youth Ministry

A strong youth ministry is discipleship based. Its leaders explain clearly how one comes to know Christ personally. They ground teens in the basics of the faith. This takes place when kids are taught to dig into God's Word. They learn it is an incredibly practical book speaking to their everyday fears, to their relationship problems, to their futures. Ultimately, when they leave home their confidence must be in the authority of the Word of God—not in a parent, not even in a youth minister, but in a heavenly Father who they have learned loves them and speaks to them practically from the Bible.

What Would It Look Like?

A strong youth ministry will have good music, often led by students with guitars, bass guitars, and drums.

Good, clean fun is important. A vital youth ministry will not be one where teens sit in dress clothes in stiff chairs and read church doctrine. Crazy skits and silly games (especially for younger teens) will attract kids. A spirit of joy should mark a believer's fellowship!

This ministry will provide a place where our kids can meet other kids who are seeking to grow in Christ. Young adults may serve as volunteer leaders meeting with small groups of teens for Bible study, sharing, and prayer. These role models who the teens think are "cool" can say things Mom and Dad can't. Laura, a twenty-four-year-old who leads a discipleship group of girls, said to Kay, a high school senior, "Should you be dating this guy? What are you going to do about it?" Kay might not have listened if her mother had said that, but she listened to Laura.

Jeff Taylor, our youth minister who had our boys in a small discipleship group for several years, would ask our son Chris, "How have your times with the Lord been lately? What's been the hardest thing for you in your thought life this week?"

He led them in a study of Jerry Bridges' *Pursuit of Holiness*. He talked with them about sex, parents, pressures, fears, and spiritual doubts. They shared their fears with him, and they listened to his advice. He has been a huge influence in our sons' "owning" their faith.

A good youth ministry will be a place in which evangelism is taking place. Teens are coming to faith in Christ and reaching out to others in their schools.

The purpose of a good ministry is *not* to keep kids busy and out of trouble. Too often the focus of a ministry is on activity—lots of events. But entertainment and activity will not equip them for life. A good youth ministry will be lots of fun, but at its core the focus will be on equipping the teens with knowledge of the relevancy of God's Word to their lives, a hunger for obedience, and a desire to share Christ with others. When evaluating a youth ministry, ask, Are the kids growing in Christ, or are they merely being entertained?

Keeping teens busy will not last. Activity will not equip them for life—a growing relationship with Christ will.

What If There's No Strong Youth Ministry in My Area?

If there is not a youth ministry in your town, be willing to start one. Pray, pray, pray and be willing to sacrifice your own time and financial resources to get one going. No matter how firm a foundation you have given your kids, they still need to hear it from someone other than Mom or Dad. Other people's influence is a crucial piece in the process of our kids "owning" their faith.

When we moved to Virginia, there was not a vital ministry in our own church or in our community. Several of us moms began to meet weekly to pray for our kids and to ask God for a good youth ministry. For weeks and months we prayed and did research. In time we raised finances and hired a Young Life worker to begin a ministry in our high school. Yes, the ministry was small. No, it never grew into great success. (In time a strong church youth ministry filled the need.) But in the early days it did disciple a handful of kids. It gave them a place with positive peer influence to get them on the right path.

What about Church?

How do we respond when our child says church is boring and he wants to sleep in on Sunday? How do we respond when our child says school is boring and he doesn't want to go? We say, "I'm sorry; we understand, but you must go anyway."

Education is important. It's not an option. If we say school is important but church is optional, we are communicating that *education is vital but God is not.* That is what the child hears. If we drop our kids off at church and go elsewhere ourselves, we are communicating that church is important for kids but optional for adults. They hear, *God is important when we are young but not necessary for adults.* Making a child go to church will not turn him off from God any more than forcing a child to go to school will turn him off from education for life.

Teens are very observant and will be quick to point out hypocrisy. Sometimes they are right. Make church a non-negotiable in your family all the way through high school. Finishing high school is family policy. So is going to church. If it's family policy and not optional from the beginning, you will not have as many Sunday morning battles. It's just a given. We go, even if we do sleep through the sermon.

"But it's boring." That is probably true to some degree. But when did boredom become a sin? We are raising kids in a dangerous culture with an "entertain me" mentality, a culture that says, "To be entertained is your right." Wrong. God has called us to give up our rights and to love Him first and our neighbors second. He has not called us to be entertained.

Seek a lively church where the preaching is biblically based, where music enhances worship, and where people are coming to Christ and serving others. You will not find a perfect church. There isn't one. Become personally involved in at least one aspect of church life outside of Sunday morning worship. It's easy to say, "But I don't get anything out of it." Instead ask, "What am I putting into it?"

What if my child goes to youth group? Isn't that enough? For most teens the answer is no. Why? Church is one of the few places where you are in fellowship with people of all ages. One of the few places where there is (or should be) social, economic, political, and racial diversity. It is the only place that cares for you from birth until death. Even if your teen says he's not getting anything, he is. Isaiah reminds us that God's Word does not return empty (Isa. 55:11). The Scripture he hears at church is at work in his subconscious. Wherever he goes when he leaves home, there is likely to be a church. If he has grown up with the habit of going to church, he will be more likely to seek one later to attend as an adult.

Sometimes you may have an older teen with whom you are struggling on many fronts. With this teen you may have to loosen up. You may have to give him a choice between youth group and church, allowing him to choose one each week. God will give you wisdom as you discern what is best in your situation (James 1:5).

You may have a spouse who is not a believer and doesn't go to church. How you handle this will depend upon your marriage relationship. Sally's husband is not a believer. Sally has not tried to force her faith on him. She prays for him and loves him. He knows that church is important to her. She has asked him to be supportive of her and to support her taking the kids. Even though he doesn't believe, he encourages the kids to go with their mom. He thinks it's good for them, and he knows it means a lot to Sally.

Be Alert to Cults

Teens today have a hunger for spiritualism. It's evident in their music, in their writings, in their searchings. Their hunger makes them open to interacting with sincere followers of Christ, but it can also make them vulnerable to dangerous cults. One cult making inroads into high schools today is called Wicca.

A form of witchcraft, Wicca focuses on feminine deity, nature worship, and self-empowerment, while rejecting more traditional faith, which is viewed as male dominated, environmentally unfriendly, and morally limiting. In Wicca there are no absolutes, no right or wrong. Instead, there is the promise of power, of believing oneself to be divine. Wiccans participate in casting of spells and customized recitations, and they encourage multiple sexual partners. Wicca attracts primarily white, well-educated teenage girls. One estimate shows between three million and five million active members today. Hollywood feature films with hip actresses and trendy

TV shows depict witches as "cool," further wooing girls in search of meaning.

Jess, a high school Wiccan, says, "Life is terrifying, and death is terrifying. You have to look for something in between. I need to believe in something." Jess is one of the many who have found Wicca on the Internet. Currently there are over three thousand pagan sites on the web.[1]

Wicca is but one of the many postmodern religions springing up in the twenty-first century. We must ask ourselves, *Where is my teen looking to fill a spiritual void in her life?*

Today it's Wicca; tomorrow it will be something else. Know what is going on in your teen's world. Stay up on the growth of new cults. Discuss their beliefs. Watch for signs of involvement on your teen's part and take steps to end her involvement. It can be a matter of life or death.

Connect Kids with Believers

One of the most crucial roles we play during the teen years is that of *connector*. We have to ask ourselves, *What vital believers can I expose my kids to? Where can I send my kids that will expose them to peers and older role models who are seeking to follow Christ?*

Invite interesting believers to have dinner with your family. Ask them to share their faith story. Your teens may groan at having to sit through a family meal, but they will hear stories of a practical, faithful, loving God. And they will hear it from someone other than Mom or Dad.

Arrange for your teen to job shadow someone in her field of interest. Shelly is interested in writing. Her mom arranged for her to spend some time with a believer in the field of journalism. This writer was able to share her faith as well as her writing tips with Shelly. And a new friendship has begun between a young writer and a teenage girl, a friendship with rich dividends for both.

Ann's sons are eighteen and sixteen. Both are avid musicians, writing and composing. Yes, they are asking tough questions about the faith. And they don't want to hear answers from their mom. During spring break, their mom arranged for them to spend several days with Chris, a young man studying computer graphics in grad school. Chris is working on a video for a class and has asked Ann's boys to help write the music for his video. A vital believer, Chris engages the boys in discussions about faith. He and his wife, Holly, are young, they love teens, and they are having a great impact on Ann's boys at this age. They are filling a gap that Ann cannot fill.

Part of the role of the body of Christ is to stand in the gap for one another. Be willing to seek the help of others. And be available to *be* that person who will stand in the gap for someone else's teen.

One of the best ways to expose our teens to other vital believers is to make wise use of their summers.

Establish a Vision for Summers

Summer is a gift of time. Our teen will not have many future summers for optional use. It's a short season in our teen's life. A wise parent will view these two and a half months as a gift and ask God for wisdom in the best way to make them count.

Each of our five children went all the way through public schools. We felt it important to use a portion of each summer for their spiritual nourishment. Our Yates family goal was to have each of our teens during their high school years participate in our church's youth ministry, attend a Young Life Camp and a FOCUS conference, and participate in a missions trip. I can honestly say that these experiences had a far greater impact in helping our kids own their faith than did anything that we, their parents, said. Did they go willingly? No, not to begin with. When we sent Allison off to the camp I mentioned earlier, she did not want to go at all. We insisted because we knew it was right, even if it was difficult for all of us initially. However, once it became clear that this was our family policy and once Allison, our eldest, reported back with enthusiasm to her younger siblings, the younger ones didn't protest as much when their turn came.

It can be helpful to send a friend along with your child to a summer camp. Most camps have scholarship help available. I've enclosed a list of summer experiences we recommend in the Resources section at the end of the book.

Our kids need to be exposed to believers from diverse backgrounds. Getting to know vital believers of different races and social, political, and economic backgrounds gives our teens a bigger picture of who God is and a greater confidence in His reality. And they learn that there is not only one type of believer.

Both youth groups and summer camps provide a place for teens to meet members of the opposite sex who can be a healthy influence. Jay, an older teen, recently spent time with two girls who are strong believers—not to mention beautiful and fun loving. After getting to know these girls, he commented to his mom, "Mom, I used to just want to marry a girl who doesn't smoke. Now that's not enough."

Too many teens just want someone to love them, and it's easier for them to lower expectations rather than to set a high standard. Older role models raise the standard and give our kids a vision for what they can have and should *wait* to find. Dean, a family friend five years older than Allison, developed a special friendship with her when she was eighteen. His authentic faith, commitment to purity, and fun-loving nature raised the standards for our daughter. Our son Chris has close friends Rob and Nate. These older boys have a deep-seated faith, and knowing them has raised the bar for our daughters, several years younger.

What about summer jobs? Shouldn't our child work in the summer? We have to weigh the needs of the family and the needs of the child for each particular summer. It's important to determine if our child should work so he can buy the *wants*: a car, label clothes, CDs, and the like, or to provide for genuine needs: things like food and family rent. Consider the possibility of your son or daughter working for part of the summer and taking time off for spiritual nourishment. Or combine both and have him get a job at a Christian camp.

If your child works, think carefully about which job he chooses. Ask, What is the purpose of the job? Will this job encourage or discourage his faith? Why work in a video store where he will be overdosed with the visual images of violence and sex all day long? Wouldn't it be better to work in a different type of retailing? Choose a job that protects Sunday worship time. Remember, you are establishing patterns for the future. If you believe work is more important than worship, what are you communicating that you value most?

When you consider the gift of summers, remember that you are the parents. You can call the shots for their summers. You have long-range perspective, and you know that these are a few crucial months in which you can take opportunities to expose your teens to others who will be instrumental in encouraging them to own their faith.

Shift from Direct Teaching to Personal Sharing

Just because our teens are most influenced by their peers doesn't mean we abdicate spiritual nourishment as a family. Rather, we see it from a different perspective. With toddlers and small children our position was that of teacher. With teens it's more a rapport of sharing with them, of growing together in faith. In a sense it's now a corporate journey. Our teens are not just our children but our younger brothers and sisters in Christ. The only thing we have over them is age, wisdom, perspective, and perhaps a few more years of knowing God. Now we have a fresh opportunity of growing side by side in our relationships with Christ. But the prospect of growing together can feel scary and raise questions for us.

What if I don't know very much myself? Our teens don't expect us to know everything. In fact, they are likely to respond positively to a dad who says, "I don't know very much about the Bible, but I'm willing to learn with you. Would you be willing to do a study with me?"

What if I don't live as I should? Be honest. Our kids aren't looking for perfect parents but for honest parents. A mom who says, "I lost my temper. Will you forgive me? Will you pray for me to get my temper under control?" will have a far greater impact on a teen's faith than a mom who acts as if she's never wrong.

What if my teen isn't interested? Try to discern what's behind their lack of interest. Does he have genuine questions? One son shared with his dad, "I've tried to believe and I've prayed for God to show me Himself, and He hasn't." This wise father encouraged his son. He promised that he would pray every day for God to reveal Himself to his son, and that he had the confidence that He would.

Is your daughter attracted to worldly lifestyles? One eighteen-year-old girl was asked, "Is it the truth of the gospel you have trouble with, or the lifestyle it calls us to live?" Her quick response, "Oh, it's the lifestyle."

Is their disinterest a way of rebelling against their parents? As you discern their questions, ask God to give you wisdom in how to respond to your particular child. He will guide you.

Sharing in God's Word together, praying together, and recommending helpful tools to each other will encourage a corporate faith.

Share God's Word

When Rich's sons were twelve and fourteen, he decided it would be good to do a Bible study with them. He chose the Book of Proverbs, because it was intended to be a book of instruction for young Hebrew men. Each of them studied the same chapter of Proverbs independently and wrote down three or four verses that he identified as important or relevant to his life. They met together every few weeks to share their verses, explaining what the verses meant to them and why they had chosen those verses. The boys began to see the Bible as a source of practical, effective guidance, and they forged new man-to-man bonds with their dad as he shared with them what he was learning.

In a house full of teens, there may not be time for a daily family study. That's okay. Instead, pray that your teen would develop the habit of a daily personal quiet time. Use special opportunities for family studies. Vacations can be a special time for a family study.

When you take a family vacation at home or to somewhere special, take along new colored pens and bright new journals for each child. Be sure everyone has a modern translation of the Bible that's theirs to mark up. The difference between reading and studying the Bible is a pen and paper. We want to encourage our kids to write down what they are learning.

When our teens were young, we went to the beach. Each day, we looked at Bible passages that had to do with the sea. One evening after studying the story of Jonah, we experienced a huge storm. We turned out all the lights in the house and huddled together to watch the lightning blaze and listen to the pounding of an angry surf. Jonah's predicament came alive in a most dramatic way. "Wow," gasped our preteen, "now I know why Jonah was scared."

As our kids became older and slept late on vacation, Johnny simply posted a passage on the refrigerator for each of us to study at our leisure during the day. We shared what we learned over dinner. One year the kids had friends at the beach, and we had teens pair up to create and lead a devotional each evening. Family times will be "more acceptable" and far richer if we let the teens lead us. Last summer, with our kids ages twenty to twenty-seven, everyone had their own Bible studies. Family dinners became a time when we had one person share "something God's been teaching me this past year."

What if my teen is resistant? How you handle this will depend upon your relationship with your child, his age, and the number of children in your family. If you have several children, persist with family times. Insist the recalcitrant one join in, but give him permission to sit quietly. It is family time. He is a part of the family. Love the struggling teen. Don't isolate him. Most of our children will go through times when they are disinterested. Let the child who is the most open take the lead. From year to year this is likely to be a different child. If you are the parents of an only child, your challenge will be more difficult. Sometimes having a friend along will make it easier. They'll join in to be polite.

What if my spouse isn't interested? You can take leadership. Do a study with the children by yourself. Invite the disinterested spouse to sit in. You can either become bitter because you have to lead since he or she won't, or you can grow in unconditional love. Your attitude will make a huge difference. Most people, even nonbelievers, are willing to tell you things you can pray about for them. It's vital to love the resistant child or spouse, to resist bitterness, and to leave them in God's hands.

What if I'm a single parent? You can still do this yourself. You can also ask another family to join you for a family study for a designated period of time. You will be encouraged if you meet with a two-parent family with kids close in age to yours. And your children will benefit from the model of a healthy marriage.

What is our goal in sharing God's Word? Our goal is that our kids would learn and experience the power and the comfort of the Word of God. That they would become convinced that this (not Mom or Dad) is the ultimate authority for how they should live.

Pray that your children would begin to have their own private daily quiet times. This is not something you should enforce or check up on. It's something you model by doing it yourself and something you pray for. When you lead a family quiet time on vacations, you give your children a picture of what they can continue on their own when you return home.

Share Prayer Requests

Vacations and special times provide us with an opportunity to share, but what about day in and day out?

Go around the breakfast table. Let every person share one thing on their schedule for the day for which they need prayer. Have each person pray for one other person. This takes about five minutes.

If someone doesn't want to pray, relax. It's okay. They can sit quietly while others pray. It's politeness to God. Include the struggling teen. Don't segregate him.

Be sure to share your needs with your kids. Early one morning the phone rang. It was Allison calling from college. "Mom, I've been praying for your writing today, and I just want to encourage you." I had been having a very bad few days, and she gladdened my heart!

Ever since our kids were tiny, Johnny and I have taken a couple of days away in August to discuss the needs of each of our children in five areas of growth: spiritual, mental, physical, emotional, and social. We write out our thoughts, and these needs and goals become our prayers for our kids for the coming year.[2]

When our children reached the teen years, we began to do this together as a family. Each family member takes time to write out his own needs and goals for the coming year, and then we get together and share with one another. We aren't asking each other for input—we are merely sharing our personal prayer requests for the next year. In the process, we gain a real insight into each other's lives, and we learn how to pray specifically for one another.

Of course, when I announced, "We're doing needs and goals next weekend. Y'all be ready," there were groans and choruses of, "Do we have to?" Laughing, I replied, "Oh, yes, it's a terrible burden of being a Yates."

At age fifteen one of Libby's emotional needs was that she not get so worried over little things. Another was that she not save things until the last minute. At age sixteen, Susy wanted to stop worrying so much about what others think. In her mental category she desired to keep up on world events by reading one news magazine each week. Chris at seventeen wanted to maintain a sense of humor and not take himself so seriously.

When Libby was seventeen, her spiritual desire was for a regular quiet time. Her goal was to spend thirty minutes alone with God each day. Another was that she would pray every day for her friend, Leslie, who was being pulled away from God. Today, four years later, Leslie has just returned from sharing Christ and caring for orphans for eight months on the mission field.

An emotional need regularly on my list is that God would control my imagination. That I would worry less and trust more. My kids pray for me in this, especially when they are late coming in!

Each year someone has the physical goal of flossing their teeth every day! Our son John added clipping nose hairs!

My husband shared one year his desire to learn how to use the computer. It's taken three years and lots of help from his staff, but he's learning!

Our friends Scott and Elise have done a family retreat for the last four years with their two sons. Elise says it's the highlight of their year. The year of their third retreat, their son Troy burst into tears as he began to share his emotional needs. It seemed he had resentment in his heart for his dad, which came pouring out. He hadn't felt listened to or affirmed by his dad as much as he wanted. His dad was totally unaware that he was impacting his son in this manner. Instead of reacting, he was able to hear his son out and to ask for forgiveness. It was the beginning of a new communication and friendship between the two of them.

Yes, your kids will roll their eyes and groan if you try this. But do it anyway. It's worth it. And one day you might be vindicated! A few years ago when I announced the upcoming day for our family sharing, John (then seventeen) responded, "I beat you, Mom. Here are mine!" And he proceeded to give each of us his computer printout of needs and goals. Recently Allison (now twenty-eight) was asked to speak to a young couples group. "What are you speaking on?" I asked.

"Oh, Mom, you are going to laugh. It's needs and goals!" she said.

Share Helpful Tools

One of the blessings of the teen years is that we can share resources. Ask your kids what books they'd recommend you read. Susy gave me a book by Max Lucado and said, "Mom, you really need to read this." I did! Ask their opinion of books. I just had three of my kids read *Finding the Love of Your Life* by Neil Clark Warren so they could tell me if I should recommend it. It was good for them to read, and their comments were helpful to me. (They do recommend it!)

Encourage your teens to take advantage of research papers to do a study on faith-related subjects. Supply them with thoughtful, intellectual, biblically based research materials.

Use summers for reading. Schools have reading lists. Why not families? We created one for our high school kids and our college kids. They include a variety of good Christian books from apologetics to fun novels.

Pray, Pray, Pray for Your Teens

When I had young children, I used to wonder why parents of older kids seemed to need to pray so much more. After all, I had good resources, creative energy, and I could "fix" most things for my young children. But it's hard to "fix" a teen. Even the greatest book, the wisest counselor, the best intentions don't always work. The older our kids get, the more we realize our best and often only resource is prayer. It's humbling, especially for us Type A people. I feel I *should* be able to fix things for this child. But the real source of my struggle is my pride. I have to come to the place where I fall on my knees and say, "God, I can't fix this situation, this teen. I desperately need You."

And I think God cheers when He hears me say, "I can't." Often, all I can do is to pray. I go to God not because of who I am or am not but because of who He is. He is the God for whom nothing is impossible (Luke 1:37).

As I pray, I remember that God answers in three ways—yes, no, or wait. He always answers out of love. He does what is best, not necessarily what is fast. He knows my child better than I do, and He loves her more than I do. He is at work in my child's life even if I can't see it. His ways are different from mine (Isa. 55:8–9). He is not limited by my timetable. He knows the future He has prepared for my child (Jer. 29:11–14). He can use anything for good in my child's life and in mine (Rom. 8:28).

The disciples asked Jesus to teach them only one thing. They asked Him to teach them how to pray. And He gave them the Lord's Prayer. Often I ask, "Oh, Lord, please teach me how to pray for this child."

Some of the things I've prayed for my teens over the years include: they would fall in love with the Word of God, they would recognize temptation and run from it, they would learn to make wise choices, if they are doing anything wrong they'd get caught, they'd learn to ask forgiveness from God and others and to receive it, that God would send strong role models their way, that God would be preparing mates for them who know and love Him first, they would remain sexually pure until marriage, they'd develop close friendships with their parents and with their siblings, they'd be thoughtful of others, they'd have a teachable spirit, and they would not be devastated by failure but instead learn from it.

It's helpful to have others praying for your child. Godparents, grandparents, and extended family members. Friends and neighbors can pray as well. I have four friends in Pennsylvania who pray and fast one day each week for all their children.

God will hear us as we pray, and He will answer in His time in His way. He longs for our teens to know Him even more than we do.

Focus Questions

Meditate on Exodus 15:1–21.

1. In this passage we see Moses' and Miriam's joy and relief that God has brought the Israelites through the Red Sea. Through this difficult season, they have seen the character of God in a fresh way. List God's character traits that they remind you of in this passage.
2. How is this season of parenting teens impacting your faith? What character trait of God do you need to remember and to focus upon?
3. What is God teaching you through your teen? (Remember they are His tools in your life.)
4. What steps can you take over the next month to expose your children to vital believers?
5. Make a list of specific things you want to pray for your teen. Divide your list into six days and pray for different items each day of the week, leaving Sunday for worship. (You might use the five areas of growth: spiritual, mental, emotional, social, and physical, to organize your prayers. What are your child's needs in each of these areas for the coming year?)

Meditate on Psalm 103. Think about how God sees you.

> In your unfailing love you will lead
>   the people you have redeemed.
> In your strength you will guide them
>   to your holy dwelling.

Exodus 15:13

9

Finding Hope When Things Don't Turn Out

I never thought "it" would happen to me.

Missy

It was the end of a long week. Getting five kids settled into school, wading through "back to school" information papers, deciding to give "the impossible teacher" a chance, praying with an apprehensive child, sorting out who had to have a car when. September can be a difficult month! Finally it was Friday. The first football game was over, their high school senior, Missy, was home, and two exhausted parents were in bed.

A blaring, persistent phone ringing jolted the parents from a sweet, deep sleep into a bitter realization that was going to change their lives forever.

"At first I thought someone had died," Jane recalled. Don, who had reached for the phone, wasn't saying much. When he did speak, he sounded extremely solemn. Hanging up the phone, he turned to Jane and said, "We have a problem. Sam just called and said that his daughter Kelly told him that Missy is pregnant. She has an appointment for an abortion tomorrow."

Jane laughed out loud in total disbelief. "No way! She's not even dating someone steadily. Her most recent beau was a counselor at a Christian camp. Besides, she's a believer, and she knows what's right and what's wrong." Yet Don seemed certain of the information he'd just received.

"We woke Missy up and asked her to come talk with us. My heart was pounding, and I felt like I was going to throw up as she walked sleepily into our room. When we told her what we'd just heard, she showed no reaction. Instead, she told us that someone had started rumors about her. I wanted to believe her, but Don did not let up with the direct questioning. Finally she just gave in and said, 'Okay, it's true.'

"I felt like I'd been socked straight in the stomach," Jane recalled. "I could see that Don was struggling with his response and the need to remain calm. We held her close and let her talk. We really didn't get too much of the story out at that point. We were all too close to the edge. We simply told her how much we loved her and would stand by her. We made her promise not to keep the appointment for the abortion the next day. Instead, we made plans together to call a close Christian friend who worked at a crisis pregnancy center.

"Although we tried, sleep didn't come. Turbulent emotions overwhelmed us. How could this have happened? How did we miss the signs? Where did we go wrong? What in the world will we do? How will this impact our other four kids? And in the midst of the questions was a huge, dull pain. This isn't the way it was supposed to be."

The next morning was the beginning of a very long journey. Months of counseling for Missy and for the whole family. Many appointments with school personnel. Tearful conversations with friends and family. Difficult decisions to make. Jane and Don had to learn that not everyone could understand or offer helpful advice. They had to let some comments go and not fret over an individual's response.

"We learned that God would show us specifically what He wanted us to do. It would be different from how He might lead another family in a similar situation. We experienced God's unique leading for us as Missy chose to make an adoption plan, and He led us to a wonderful Christian couple. Today, when we visit our grandson with his parents and little sister, we marvel at God's faithfulness in bringing good out of a difficult situation."

Today as a college junior, Missy reflects, "Although this was a horrible time for me and my parents, today we are closer than we ever were. Before this happened, I was not honest with my parents. Now I feel I can tell them anything. I don't have to worry about hiding something from them. We've been through too much together."

Mac

Sally had just about finished baking her famous chocolate chip cookies. Cooking had always brought her joy, but today her joy was tinged with a sense of uneasiness. She knew that her husband, Jim, was worried about Mac, their eighteen-year-old who was away at school. Recently when he'd been home, he'd seemed distant, uncooperative. He didn't want to talk. He stayed out later and later and was unusually secretive about what he was doing. And his new friends made them feel uneasy. But he was a good kid, and they'd always been close as a family. "Jim's probably overreacting," she reasoned as she put more cookies in the oven.

A phone call from the police station blew apart Sally's fantasy world. Mac and some friends had been to a concert, where he'd bought a large quantity of marijuana. When they left the concert, they were drinking. An alert policeman saw the guys drinking while driving, pulled the car over, and arrested the boys. Now they were in jail, where they would remain for the night.

Although caught completely off guard, Sally's first reaction was to pray. She'd always prayed that her boys would get caught if they were doing anything wrong, and this was truly an answer to prayer. She sensed God's protection, and out of years of habit she turned immediately to Him.

Jim, on the other hand, was both sad and relieved. "It felt like an expected death," he said. "The mystery and the suspicion were removed; now we had to deal with reality." Initially Jim and Sally were angry. Angry with Mac for violating their trust. Angry for all the lies he had told them. Angry that he had not appreciated all that had been given to him and done for him. But there was also guilt. "Why is this happening to us? Where did we go wrong?"

Jim and Sally grieved differently. Sally cried and Jim became solitary. Sally wanted to sleep all the time. Grief physically exhausted her. But in their pain, they made an important decision together.

"We are not going to let this tear apart our marriage. We will not let this crisis have that kind of power over us. It has already done enough damage. We refuse to let 'us' become a casualty too."

When Mac was arrested, Jim immediately put on his "fix-it hat" and went to work finding the best counselors. A wise counselor made it clear that Mac's problem was worse than he'd led his parents to believe; he had been abusing alcohol and drugs since he was fourteen. There was no "quick fix." Mac entered an inpatient rehabilitation hospital for thirty-nine days, followed by five months in a halfway house. The whole family began counseling.

Recently we took a mission trip with Mac and his family. During our journey, we celebrated Mac's birthday and his nearly nine years of sobriety. When I asked Mac about that crisis time in his life and these ensuing years, he quickly responded, "When those policemen arrested me, I knew I was in big trouble. However, at the same time, there was a surprising sense of relief. My secret was out. I no longer had to hide. It was the beginning of recovery."

Christie

"Christie has always been such a strong person," remarked her mother. "I would never have imagined in a hundred years that she would have an eating disorder. Why, I remember the two of us sitting at the kitchen table laughing about an article we had just read about the high rate of female athletes with eating disorders. We both roared and said, 'That could never happen to either of us.' We couldn't have been more wrong."

The number two singles tennis player in the state of Texas, Christie was recruited by top universities across the country. The University of Virginia won her heart, and she packed her bags to head "north."

Unusually disciplined, Christie arrived at school determined to excel athletically, academically, and socially. Along with most freshmen, she began to put on weight. Girls joked about the "freshman fifteen"—fifteen pounds students often gain their first year. When Christie realized she'd quickly gained five pounds, she decided that her daily tennis practice wasn't enough, and she began to work out even more. Her exercise became the focal point of her day. And her thoughts about food consumed her. By Christmas her weight had dropped considerably, and when she went home, many people complimented her on how good she looked. Encouraged by this affirmation from others, Christie increased her exercise and began to eat less and less. When her mom, Sue, went up to see her play that spring, some of Christie's teammates pulled Sue aside and said they were worried about her daughter's weight loss. There was talk of a possible eating disorder. The coach told Sue that Christie must not lose any more weight over the summer. In fact, she needed to gain.

Concerned, Sue talked with her daughter. They'd always been open about everything. They'd been tennis partners and friends as well as mother and daughter. At this point Christie said she didn't think she had a problem, but she'd be careful. She didn't want an eating disorder. She believed she could control it. Satisfied with their conversation, Sue told the coach she'd make sure Christie didn't lose any more weight over the summer.

But it wasn't that easy. Christie was teaching tennis and working out nonstop. She became grouchy and testy. Little things made her angry, and she didn't want her mom talking to her about food. Tension filled a once happy home.

"I saw my strong daughter become a vulnerable waif, and I couldn't help her. It was a really awful summer," Sue recalled.

With her return to school in the fall, her tennis coach, Phil, took one look at her and sent her to a psychologist in the eating disorder clinic at the university. Here she heard the shocking words, "Christie, you clearly have an eating disorder called anorexia nervosa."

"I was devastated," Christie remembers. "I felt so defeated and so responsible at the same time. I felt like a bad person and a failure before God. Since I was a believer, I thought I should have been able to prevent this or at least to pray my way out of it."

The first several months of counseling with the psychologist and meeting with the nutritionist were really hard.

"I felt like I was trapped behind bars. Every day I had to bear the burden of fear and anxiety about what I ate and how much I was able to exercise. At first I couldn't even say out loud, 'I'm anorexic.' That felt like an admission of defeat, of saying I'd done this to myself. But when I began to be honest about my disease, I began to experience real freedom."

Christie's mom was relieved to have a definitive diagnosis and to have some help. They had always dealt with things in their family. And now there was something specific to deal with. Yet it was hard for her as she asked herself, *How did this happen? Have I in some way been responsible? Both*

Christie and I are perfectionists. I want things to be just right, and I know I want to control things. Maybe if I'd loosened up, maybe if . . .

Even today Sue doesn't have all the answers, but that's not important. She has realized that this disease isn't something you can take an antibiotic for and be healed in ten days. Instead, anorexics will have a lifetime challenge of looking at themselves from a new perspective. She, too, has learned a lot through counseling, and as she and Christie have worked through this together, they have grown closer to each other.

Christie has realized that she had believed lies from the enemy. Lies our culture tells us. Lies like if you are thin, you are valuable. If you are disciplined, you are worthy. If you are beautiful, you are acceptable. If you are thinner, people will like you more. Christie had to learn to hear God's voice instead of the enemy's lies.

"One day I made a list of all the lies I knew I believed, and then I wrote down God's truths about me, and this helped me realize how distorted my thinking had become," Christie recalled. Some of the truths Christie discovered are included in the notes at the end of this book.[1]

Now a healthy college senior, Christie looks back on this difficult time in her life as a blessing.

"Even though this has been the hardest thing I've ever been through, God used it to break me. He's shown me that I do have real weaknesses, and it's okay. He's used it to help me connect better with other people who are struggling with problems. I find that people talk to me more than before, because they know I don't have it all together. No one does, but it's hard to believe that in today's culture."

Rob

Sports were Rob's passion. And he was really good. Even as a freshman, he won a spot as tight end on the varsity football team of his large public high school, a school accustomed to winning state championships. His whole family was proud of Rob, and his parents were his biggest cheerleaders, rarely missing a game. Rob's dream, his goal in life, was to play football for the military academy at West Point. His sophomore year he was a top scorer and the leading pass receiver on the team, as well as excelling in academics. The summer after his sophomore year, he attended the football sports camp at the Naval Academy. His many years of hard work began to pay off, and he was noticed and applauded by the coaches. His life's dream seemed closer to reality.

His first day home from sports camp, he headed off for a scrimmage with his high school team. Full of confidence, Rob jumped high in the air to receive a pass. As he landed, he felt something go "pop" in his left knee.

Days later after many tests, the orthopedist delivered the crushing news, "You've severed your anterior cruciate ligament [the ACL, the main ligament that stabilizes the knee]. You won't be able to play football for at least a year and maybe never, and you'll have to go through extensive rehabilitation."

Rob was devastated, but the pain for his mom and dad was in some ways more intense, for they had the pain of their own disappointment coupled with the incredible pain a parent feels for their child's loss. It was a double whammy. And their son was so special. A committed believer, he had given his life to walking with God. He'd resisted temptation.

He'd excelled in academics, in sports, and in leadership at his school. It just didn't seem fair.

His dad's pain was intense because of his own love of football. He identified with his son's intense loss of this love. But the pain went deeper than that. It brought forth the piercing question of God's faithfulness. His son walked with God. Even as an underclassman, he led his teammates in prayer. In the frequently hostile environment of a large public high school, he was uncompromising in his testimony. He had been faithful to God, but God . . . ?

Rob determined to come back. After surgery, he spent his entire junior year rehabilitating his knee. When his teammates went to practice, he went to rehab—four long, painful hours every day. Every weekend he sat on the bench encouraging his teammates.

Life was hard, and it was lonely.

Rob's mom instinctively understood his loneliness. Not only was her pain caused by the loss of her son's dream and by the sight of his physical pain, but she also saw his loneliness. She knew he felt left out of the locker-room camaraderie. She ached over those long, solitary hours of rehab.

Just before his senior year, he was cleared by the doctor to play again. Maybe his hard work had paid off. His dream flickered on the horizon once more.

The night of his first preseason game was to be a great celebration. His whole family and many friends turned out to cheer for him. On the first play he cut back to cover someone, and his other knee went "pop" as he fell to the ground. No one had even touched him. He recognized the pain. He knew. It couldn't be. *Please, God, don't let it be!* But it was. He had torn his ACL in the good knee. His football days were over. His dream had died.

Rehab was far more difficult this time. The same intense pain, the daily isolation, but now there was no dream to work for.

Once again the family pulled together. They wept together, prayed together. And they clung to God in the midst of hard questions: *Why, God? What's the point? Did I hear You wrong? I thought I was following You. Are You really sovereign, God? Are You really a good God? Where are You, God?*

Difficult questions with no pat answers.

Disappointment. Pain. Loss of a dream.

Almost two years have passed since the end of Rob's football dream. Today he attends the University of Virginia, where he was awarded an ROTC scholarship. He's living with several Christian guys, growing in his faith, and continuing to process the lessons learned in a painful season.

Whether it's the result of sin, poor choices, or circumstances beyond our control, hard times will happen to us and to our kids. God's promise is not that we will avoid pain or trouble in this life, but that He will be with us in the midst of trouble.

"God is our refuge and strength, an ever-present help in trouble" (Ps. 46:1). It's helpful to picture Him in our trouble, in fact to visualize Him as a comforting shield between us and the trouble.

Emotional Responses to Pain

Whatever the cause of our pain, we'll experience several common emotions. When we recognize the following emotions and begin to work through them, we will realize we are not alone, and we will begin to receive God's comfort in a profound way.

Anger

When things don't turn out, it's so easy to be angry. And there are plenty of people around to be angry with!

Jill was furious with her son. The middle of three boys, he had been a constant source of pain. Now he had run away again. Both his older and younger brothers were so much easier to raise. But not this one—why? He had the same two parents, the same home, the same advantages, the same Christian emphasis, yet still he made poor choices. Her struggle with menopause, the loss of her mother, and tension in her marriage only served to fuel Jill's anger with her son. How could he cause her so much pain in the midst of everything else?

Sandy was angry with her husband, Larry. He was never at home. Their son was staying out late and running with a bad crowd, and she knew he was headed for trouble. Because Larry was a preacher, he felt he had to be available for his congregation. It was his calling. Sandy felt unspiritual when she begged him to stay home some evenings. "You just need to trust God, and everything will be all right," Larry would say. But everything was not all right. Their son was in deep trouble, and Sandy couldn't get through to her husband. She felt frustrated, confused, and angry.

Jack was angry with himself. Looking back over the past several years, he realized that he was the cause of many of his son's problems. He'd pushed him to excel in athletics because he had done so. He hadn't listened when his son said he didn't like sports. He pushed him to make the best grades, to try for the Ivy League schools. "You aren't trying hard enough," he'd say. But what his son heard was, "You aren't what I wanted in a son." And now his son had stormed out, told him he hated him, and revealed the fact that he was struggling with his sexual identity. Jack's anger turned inward because, as he listened to his son, he saw his own failings.

Sometimes we get angry at God. We cry out, "How could You do this to me, God? If You are a loving God, how could You let this happen? Why me? Why my child?"

David, the hero of the Israelites, often got angry with God. He too asked these same questions.

"How long, O LORD? Will you forget me forever? How long will you hide your face from me? How long must I wrestle with my thoughts and every day have sorrow in my heart?" (Ps. 13:1–2).

What do we do with our anger?

Acknowledge it. Don't pretend that it's not there. Remember, not all anger is bad. Jesus Himself was angry with the money changers in the temple. He threw the money changers out on their heels. David got angry with God. We can be angry with the drunk driver that injures our child, the teen who has repeatedly lied to us, the boy who abused our daughter. But when we let our anger turn into bitterness, we begin down a path of misery and sin.

Give your anger to God. Like David, tell God how you are feeling. He understands. In our anger we have to ask God to forgive us and to protect us from bitterness. We have to ask Him to enable us to grant forgiveness to the other person. This may be the hardest thing we ever do. And we may need help doing it. Forgiveness doesn't "make everything feel better." And forgiveness doesn't mean we have to trust the other person or put ourselves or our child in a foolish situation. But healing cannot come without the step of forgiveness. Healing takes a long time.

Eugene Peterson says

> The act of forgiveness begins by accepting the sin, whatever it is. It does not blink at the sin, it does not obscure it, it does not excuse or modify or explain it: it faces it. And it accepts the consequences of the sin. Whatever suffering, whatever penalties, whatever discomfort, whatever inconveniences proceed from the sin, they are also accepted. What else was the cross but an act of enormous courage, accepting the results of sin?[2]

Guilt

When things go wrong, we feel guilty. And often we are. Our child's problems can be because of our own sin. We all make mistakes as parents. Yes, we're guilty. But we may also take on guilt that's not ours to bear. It's not our fault that our teen chose to drink. It was his choice. Yes, things we did or didn't do may have sent him down this path, but in the end it was his choice. We cannot take all the blame.

We handle guilt in much the same way we handle anger. We are honest about our guilt. We confess it, and we receive God's forgiveness (Prov. 28:13; 1 John 1:9). There is nothing He can't forgive.

It's helpful to be aware of two traps: the trap of self-pity and the trap of a critical spirit.

Self-pity can come in the form of the "if only's." *If only I had been there. If only I'd seen the signs, if only I'd had more sup-*

port from my spouse, if only I had a spouse, if only my daughter had not been injured, if only I had listened to God, if only I had obeyed God. If only, if only . . . If you find yourself overcome with your own failure, remember Paul's words to the Romans. "Therefore, there is now no condemnation for those who are in Christ Jesus" (Rom. 8:1). The "if only's" can lead us into self-pity or into a critical spirit.

In our self-pity it's easy to look at someone else and think, *Why me? Why not her? She doesn't have any problems. Nothing bad ever seems to happen to her. It's not fair. Her life seems so perfect. Her kids haven't rebelled. She has a good husband,* and so on. We become critical of "her," and bitterness seeps in. Our critical spirit has become the sin of envy. We covet her life. But wait! We need to remember that there are always facts missing. We don't know everything about someone else's life. Everyone struggles in some area. Everyone has pain. It's not up to us to put a value on pain, to say, "Mine is greater than hers." We don't know how pain feels to someone else. What causes pain and the degree of that pain is different for every person. Pain is pain. We have to avoid wrong assumptions about someone else's life. It will only lead to a critical spirit.

Fear

Another common response to the bad things that happen is fear.

"My teen has ruined his life." Or, "I've messed up my child for life."

We feel like it's too late. But it's never too late for God, and it's never too late to do what is right. What keeps us from giving in to despair is remembering God's redeeming power. There is nothing that He cannot redeem. "For nothing is impossible with God"(Luke 1:37). He can redeem the grossest situation and bring good out of the biggest mess (Rom. 8:28).

Our fear can reveal itself in a case of the "what if's." *What if we don't make the right school choice? What if he gets injured again? What if she runs away? What if I mess up my next child too? What if he gets AIDS?*

The "if only's" drag us down as we look at the past; the "what if's" can cause us irrational fear when we imagine the future. Simply recognizing these traps will help to lessen the fear.

Perhaps you haven't had any great crises. Your challenges in raising teens have been normal. Yet just reading this chapter scares you. You fear something awful will happen in your own family. You live in fear, just waiting for bad news. I certainly struggle with this myself. It's easy to live a life of dread, to be controlled by fear. I have to continually give my fears to God. I hate this about myself. But it keeps me humble. And I am comforted by the fact that God knows I am but dust (Psalm 103). He understands. My fear has no power. God has power, and there's power in His Word.

Yes, our kids will all suffer pain, mistreatment, rejection, disappointment, and failures. They will struggle with doubt. So will we as their parents. But all teens do not have to have a major crisis. They do not have to rebel.

Five Comforts When Faced with Pain

Whether we face a major crisis or experience normal pain, the following five comforts will help us keep perspective.

1. Run to God

When Bill lost his job for the third time in ten years, it was hard on the family. Especially hard for his fifteen-year-old son, Drew. As his parents broke the news at dinner, Drew, with the arrogant air of a cynical teenager, responded sarcastically, "Well, I guess you guys will be depending on God again."

His wise mom gently responded, "Yes. We've found Him to be reliable."

Our kids watch where we run in difficult times. They observe how we handle tragedy and disappointment. They may be angry, cynical, or distant, but they are watching. One of the blessings of these teen years is that our kids begin to understand that Mom and Dad do not have control over life. We cannot make everything okay for them or for ourselves. We have disappointments too. This is a good place to be with our teens, because sometimes all we can do is to go to God *together*.

When Rob tore his ACL, the entire family gathered together. With arms wrapped around one another in tears, they simply prayed. They poured out their feelings and emotions to God. It was the only safe place to go. It was the only place of supernatural comfort.

Proverbs 18:10 says, "The name of the LORD is a strong tower; the righteous run to it and are safe." We have to ask, "In my pain, to what or to whom am I running?"

When we run to God, we begin to experience the fellowship of His sufferings. In Hebrews 2:17–18 we find out why Christ is truly the only one who can understand our pain. When we are in pain, His Word will comfort us. The Book of Psalms offers comfort in times of despair.

When we run to God, we find hope. When I am in a hard place, I practice my "principle of the other." Jeremiah 33:3 says, "Call to me and I will answer you and tell you great and unsearchable things you do not know."

I pray, "Lord, I'm in a hard place. I don't know the answers to this hard thing right now. I know You do, but Lord, You don't seem to be showing me right now. Lord, help me to leave this issue with You and wait. While I wait on You for this issue, open my eyes and teach me something great and new."

When I am in a hard place, God has my attention. It's easy to be so focused on the issue at hand that I worry instead of trust. God may have something totally unrelated to the issue to teach me during this time.

A few years ago our son Chris was struggling with an important decision. He prayed and agonized and could not get clarity. In his confusion, he became depressed. As I watched him, I agonized for him. I cried out to God over and over, begging Him to answer Chris's prayers. My response from God seemed to be silence. Feeling frustrated, I cried out to God, "Okay, You have my attention, Lord. I can't do anything about Chris right now, so please show me something else. What is the 'other' that You would say to me?"

God began to gently reveal to me that I had lost sight of who He is. In my heart and mind, the issue of Chris had become bigger than God. I realized that I needed to daily refocus on God's character. Each morning before getting out of bed, I would choose one character trait of God to think about during the day. In my Bible study I often looked up verses related to the trait. One morning I chose, "God is a rescuer," and I thought about how He loves to rescue. While fixing breakfast, my phone rang. A friend was in tears over her son.

"Susan," she said, "I just feel like he needs to be rescued."

God loves to teach us "great, other things" that will encourage and bless us. If we run to Him and ask Him to show us new things in our time of pain, He will give us a positive vision and a fresh perspective in a difficult season.

2. Protect Your Marriage

When Jim and Sally made the commitment not to let Mac's drug problem break apart their marriage, they took a step that was to be both difficult and protective. Difficult because in the following months it was easy to blame one another. "If only you had [or hadn't] . . ." It was easy to expect the other to respond in the same way, instead of allowing each other to grieve differently. The stress of the situation magnified normal marital irritations. But they continued to cling to the promise they had made. It protected their marriage by forcing them to operate as a team, a team in which each player brings different strengths and, yes, different weaknesses.

I mentioned earlier that building a marriage and a family is a bit like putting together one of those huge jigsaw puzzles. So many pieces with different sizes and shapes. Each piece has to be placed in such a way as to make the other pieces look good. And the only one who has the final picture in mind is the creator of the puzzle. Marriage is learning how to put the pieces together, how to complement our mate instead of compete, how to balance weaknesses and strengths. Just when we think we're making headway, *boom!* A crisis hits, and it's as if the puzzle gets tossed into the air and we have to begin all over again. Even if there's no big crisis, there are new seasons in life—the birth of the first child, the teen years, the empty nest. Each new season has a way of tossing up those carefully placed pieces, and we have to begin to put them together again.

In some seasons, one mate will be better able than the other to respond to a child. When our son John reached the teen years, he seemed to communicate better with his dad than with me. I sensed his withdrawing from me, and at first it hurt my feelings. But I realized it was an opportunity to take advantage of, not to resent. My husband and I talked about this open window he had at this particular time with his son. How could he capitalize on it? He asked John Jr. if he would like to go out to breakfast once a week before school to talk. He said yes, and the two men began to meet. Some days they would read the Scriptures together. Other times they shared prayer requests. In time Chris joined them. When John Jr. went to college, he wrote his dad a letter saying, "Dad, I've been looking for an older man to mentor me, and I've realized I want you. (Yes, I'll still seek out older folks here.) So what would you think of us making the commitment to write once each week and share what God is doing in our lives and what we are thinking about?"

Wow.

God has given us our mates to balance us. Often Johnny has to say to me, "Susan, you are overreacting." Frequently he's right. He's more objective. But he needs me to clue him in as to a teen's feelings. He's not as perceptive as I am.

Whether we are going through a crisis or a typical difficult time with a teen, we have to remember, "My mate is not my enemy." We are on the same team.

Remember the jigsaw puzzle that's like our marriage? Be patient—it won't be finished this side of heaven. The joy comes in the work of putting it together, not in the finished product. But the finished product is gorgeous. God designed it.

A word to those of you who may be single parents. Going through a difficult time with a teen can provide you with an opportunity for enhancing communication with the child's other parent. For once the child is the focus, not your relationship. You have to pull together for the sake of the child.

It can also be encouraging to meet with a third party for advice. By all means, if you are a single parent, ask another couple to come alongside you as you raise your teens. A two-parent couple should seek to befriend a single parent and his or her kids. Both families will be blessed.

3. Get Friends to Pray and Play

Jenny Lou called Sally after Mac's arrest. "Sally," she said, "Linda and I want to meet with you every week just to pray for Mac." Both of these women knew Mac and loved him. When they met with Sally, they didn't offer advice, they didn't pray for other people. They just prayed for Mac. Sally's friends Jackie and Sue also prayed faithfully for Mac. The love of these women comforted Sally. Today, she says that she doesn't know what she would have done without these friends.

Sometimes we may be too burdened to pray for our own child. I was really worried about one of my girls. I kept praying and praying, but my praying only caused me to worry more. My friend Kim said, "It's time for you to stop praying for her for a while. I will take that burden off your shoulders and pray and fast for her. You are not to pray about this situation during this period of time."

What a gift Kim gave me. She relieved me of a burden. And God did abundantly answer her prayers. This is the way the body of Christ is supposed to work. We have to stand in the gap for each other.

Enlist friends to pray for your teens. Pray for theirs. Ask grandparents, godparents, and other extended family to pray.

We need to pray, but we also need to play. Our God is a practical God. When He healed Jairus's daughter, He didn't say, "Now go call a worship meeting in the synagogue." He said, "Give her something to eat" (Mark 5:43).

When we're having a hard time, we lose perspective. We forget to eat. We forget to play. We are too consumed with our problem. Take a friend in pain out to a delicious lunch. Go to a department store and get a makeover together. Visit a museum. Get out in nature. Play with animals and babies. Visit a nursing home. Spend time with a friend who makes you laugh. Laughter invigorates and lifts our spirits. Simply focusing our brains on something other than "our issue" will help restore our perspective.

4. Take Advantage of Good Resources

We've talked about how much teens need good role models who will care for them. But how about their parents? Who will "mother" the moms and who will "father" the dads?

If you are in a hard place with your teens, seek out a wise older couple at least a season ahead of you. Meet with them and ask their advice. Even if you are not in a difficult spot at the moment, you still need the encouragement of someone older. As you glean from their years of experience, you will be a blessing to them too.

Good Christian counseling may be necessary. But be sure you get a reference. Just because someone is a Christian doesn't mean he or she is a good counselor.

With the abundance of resources today, it is not as hard as it used to be to find someone *who has been where you are.* Part of the comfort they receive is helping you.

John and Sue Vawter have *been in a place they never expected to be.* He is the pastor of a lively church. Their kids have grown up with love and security. But a few years ago their world fell apart. They discovered that their daughter, Steff, was a heroin addict, spending at least seventy dollars per day to support her habit. Through a series of both painful and miraculous events, John and Sue were able to get Steff into a treatment center. Two years later, John hosted a conference at his church for sixty-three parents, all pastors and missionaries whose kids were abusing drugs and alcohol. These were good parents who came in search of answers to questions like, What did we do wrong?

When John and Sue asked Steff this question, she replied, "You didn't do anything wrong. You taught me right. These are choices I made."

At the conference couples received comfort from John, Sue, and Steff, and they received hope. The conference was called "You're Not Alone." Similar conferences are still being held.[3]

No one has to feel alone. Someone else has likely experienced whatever you are going through right now. If you will make the effort to connect with others *who've been there,* you will be comforted. You will find a list in the Resources section to help you in making these connections.

5. Remember God

Why was my first point "Run to God" and this last one "Remember God"? Isn't that redundant? Yes, but for me and perhaps for you it's necessary. You see, often when a hard time hits, I run to God, but then as I get into my "fix-it mode," getting friends to pray, protecting my marriage, seeking good resources, subtly, quietly, my focus becomes my plan of action. It isn't that all these steps aren't necessary. They are. It's just that it's too easy for me to forget *who He is* as I focus on what I'm doing.

The bottom line is that I want to be God. I want to fix, to control, to dictate. One of the things Mac said to his dad during their family counseling was, "Dad, you can plan the event, but you can't determine the outcome." We can't be God. What a relief.

We have to fall back on *who He is* over and over again.

Recently I was on an airplane. Emotionally, physically, and spiritually exhausted from weeks of speaking, I couldn't wait to get home and sleep in my own bed. As I thought about my kids, I began to worry about one in particular. I had some reasons to be concerned, but now as I thought about things, my imagination began to go haywire. In my exhausted state I was especially vulnerable to false assumptions. I was overcome with the "what if's." I began to pray, but that only made matters worse.

I felt guilty that I wasn't trusting God. Finally, in desperation I cried out to the Lord, "Please help me!" I did not hear an audible reply, but it was one of those times that I knew He spoke to me. What came to my mind was so unexpected. It was simply, quietly, *"Remember Me."*

In all my fretting, I had let the problem become my focus. I let it grow and grow, way out of proportion. I had forgotten who He is—the Lord of Lords, my Father who loves this teen far more than I do, the one who knows everything about this teen, the one who gently cares for this teen, the one who wants only the best for this precious child, the one with the power to change, the one for whom nothing is impossible.

When hard times come and life is confusing, we have to fall back on what we know to be true.

Is God whispering to you, *"Remember Me"*?

Focus Questions

Meditate on Psalm 77.

1. How might the words of the psalmist comfort you in a painful time with your teen? How might they comfort your teen?

2. How has a painful time impacted your relationship with Christ? Have you run to Him (Prov. 18:10)? Why or why not? What have you learned?

3. We can't raise our kids by ourselves. We desperately need others. Ask God to give you another parent (dad to dad, mom to mom) with whom you can share kid concerns. It must be someone who keeps confidences. Agree to pray regularly for one another's teens for a period of six months. Update each other weekly.

Meditate on 1 Peter 1:3–9 and 2 Corinthians 1:3–7 and be comforted.

I will remember the deeds of the LORD;
 yes, I will remember your miracles of long ago.
I will meditate on all your work
 and consider all your mighty deeds.

         Psalm 77:11–12

10

Helping Teens Choose the Right College or Job

How am I supposed to know?

The knot in my stomach was tightening. The closer April 1 got, the more anxious I got. And I was just the mother! My daughter was edgy, but she was also just tired of the process and wanted it to be over. We had waited all spring for this day, the day "it" would arrive. If "it" was a fat letter, that meant good news, but if "it" was slim, then the news was bad!

April 1 is both a dreaded and anticipated day for parents of high school seniors. It's the official day that college acceptances and rejections arrive in the mail. And it's a stressful time for most families. As a parent you wonder how much input you should have and how much to leave up to your child. You may not have confidence in your child's decision making. And it's tough because you may not know the right answer yourself. Your child may not get into the college of your choice or his. He may not want to go to college right away. He may not want to go at all. He may have too many options or not enough choices. Adding to your confusion is all the advice coming from other people.

Scary emotions, confusing thoughts. What is right? Who is right? How do you decide? What is God's best plan for your child at this time in his or her life?

Having been through this process five times, I wouldn't want to do it again. But I have seen God's faithfulness, and I have learned a few things that will be helpful as you and your child begin to consider life after high school. Two underlying principles will be important in your planning: *this is a joint decision* and *fellowship will be crucial.*

This Is a Joint Decision

Even though our kids are graduating, they are still our children. And we need to have a say in this decision. Give your child some parameters for making the decision. Agree together on approximately five colleges to apply to. Or consider two noncollege opportunities that both you and your teen feel good about. Pray that God will make the final choice clear to your teen. Ultimately it should be her decision, but this involves a step of letting go on our part.

When Allison, our eldest, was trying to decide between three schools, she couldn't make up her mind. I prayed and prayed for God to make it clear to us where she should go, but I wasn't getting any clarity on the matter. As the deadline approached for her response, I began to complain to the Lord. *Why won't You tell me, Lord? We really need to know.*

As I prayed, I sensed God saying to me, "Susan, do not fret because I'm not telling you. I am going to show Allison. It's a part of your letting go. Wait and be encouraged as I show her." At the last minute He did show her in a very clear way. Most importantly, He showed me that I was no longer as crucial in her life. I could entrust her to Him.

Fellowship Will Be Crucial

Kids out of high school are usually seventeen or eighteen years old. Many are preparing to be on their own for the first time, often away from family and in an unfamiliar setting. They are still greatly influenced by peers. This is a transitional time in their lives, and they need a strong fellowship. It is not the time for them to stand alone in a culture, trying to make a difference without the support of a small group of solid believers. Some are not likely to seek out fellowship on their own. They may *think* they can maintain their faith and values without support, but this will not happen. No one can walk alone in today's world. Not us, not our kids. Kids, especially those on their own for the first time, need strong fellowship. At this age they are still figuring out who they are. Who they decide to be will be greatly influenced by whom they spend time with in this next year. This transitional season can be a time when their faith truly becomes their own, when they choose to believe not because of their parents or their youth group or . . . but because they want to believe. We pray that they choose to follow Christ, but if we send them to a campus or job where they are without other strong believers, they will be less likely to grow in their faith. The first two years out of high school are transition years, not a good season to be a lonely believer.

College or Work?

Some teens will not have many options. Others will be overwhelmed with too many choices. Family situations and expectations are different, and even in the same family no two children are alike. You may have one child for whom college has never been an option. His educational goal has been fulfilled with graduation from high school. Yet his younger brother may already be thinking about doctoral studies! Neither is better; they are merely different. Every teen is gifted in very specific ways. If college is not an option, help your child find a job that will encourage his natural gifts and interests to develop.

Some students may benefit by taking a year off before going to college. This is known as a "gap year." Whether it's a gap year or the end of formal education, a wise parent will make sure that this first year out of high school is spent in a situation in which the teen will be encouraged and surrounded by strong believers who will help him grow up. Playing in a band traveling around the country may *sound* like a wonderful experience, but at eighteen or nineteen your child is not yet ready to face the challenges this will bring. He needs time to mature in his faith and grow up first. In his youthful idealism, our child may *think* he can handle anything, but a parent knows that wisdom comes from experience. We do our child a great disservice if we encourage him to do something that he would be better equipped for later when he has had a few years to mature. It helps to remember that *delay is not denial.*

For a gap year, a teen might consider doing a mission project or working at a Christian conference center. Or he could take an apprentice year in his field of interest under the day-in and day-out direction of a believer. He may not make much money, but the value of a godly mentor in the marketplace is priceless.

Leslie, a young friend of mine, decided to do a gap year after graduating. She felt that she was simply not yet ready for the challenges of college life. She feared she would be pulled down in her faith, and she was unsure about her field of study. Instead, she took an internship with Youth With A Mission (YWAM), a Christian ministry. Talking with her later that year, I was astounded by her newfound personal confidence and her deepened relationship with Christ. Postponing college and spending time with believers enabled her to solidify her convictions apart from the temptations of a college setting.

Discuss the options for your teen with your mate. Seek the counsel of other adults who know him well. Listen to his desires and dreams. And pray. God has a plan, and He will lead you together.

Choosing a College—Where Do We Begin?

Rob and his mom were having a talk about college choices.

"Do you know where you want to go, Son?" she inquired.

"How am I supposed to know? I can't even decide which soft drink I want for lunch. How am I supposed to decide where to go to college?"

Choosing a college does seem like an overwhelming task, not only for our teen but also for us. With our first child, we don't know what we're doing. And as for our child—he's either really stressed about the decision or he couldn't care less.

Here are eight tips that will help to make this process an adventure rather than an agony.

1. Develop Your Own Personal Strategy

The college pressure begins much earlier today. A student's GPA begins to count in his or her ninth-grade year. It's important to begin to discuss college goals now with your child. Don't expect to have all the answers. Instead, take time to formulate questions.

Most schools have guidance counselors. Make an appointment sometime in the fall of the freshman year and go in with your child to discuss his goals with the counselor. Plot a strategy for classes he will need to qualify for the type of college in which he is interested. Let your teen take the leadership in the conversation.

Don't expect him to think this is a great idea. He'll likely complain. Complaining is "his job" at this age. But do it anyway. It sets the tone that you care about his future and shows that you want to work with him to help him realize his goals. If you both obtain accurate information about requirements, you'll be less likely to find yourself later on saying, "I wish we'd known . . ." His goals may change, but this is an important first step. Simply having a plan relieves stress.

A good guidance counselor will know what sorts of things specific colleges are looking for in applicants. She will be able to advise your child on his extracurricular activities. Today most schools are not impressed with a long list of clubs. They are more interested in a focused child who invests significant time in a few things rather than simply joining everything to build a resumé.

Resumé building can be a touchy subject. As the parent we must avoid pressuring our teen to do things simply for the sake of building his resumé. On the other hand, we do want to encourage him to take risks to develop his gifts and to make a contribution to his high school.

It's a mistake to pressure your child to excel academically or athletically, or to go to your alma mater in order to fulfill *your* dream. He is a different person than you are; God has a unique plan for him.

If we as parents are praying for the right place to be revealed, and if we approach the decision with a sense of "going on an adventure with our child," the stress will be less for everyone.

2. Determine Your Criteria

Each time we began the college search, I gave my teen a blank journal book. I wrote a personal letter in the front of it to him (or her) telling him how proud I was of him and why. Things like: I love your thoughtfulness, your leadership gifts, and the way you have persevered in tough situations. And I included promises from Scripture for him to focus on in the search process. For example: Psalm 37:23–24; Proverbs 3:5–7; Isaiah 48:17; and Jeremiah 29:11–14. I reassured him that I knew God had a special plan for him, and that God would show us what it was in His time. I reminded him of my confidence in God and in him.

Our kids used a section of the journal to formulate ten criteria that were important for them in choosing a college. Criteria like fellowship, location (city or small town), size, cost, and the type of academic challenge. Many of the criteria, like fellowship, were the same for each child, but some, like size, were different. Each time we visited a campus, our teen rated the school in each area. He also wrote down his own impressions. In the process we discovered that some criteria were more important than others, and we often made changes. If you are considering both secular and Christian colleges, it's good to visit both and record your impressions. Having everything in one book was helpful in remembering different things later on when he forgot what he felt on which campus.

If we parents have certain restrictions, it's best to communicate these in the beginning of the process. Ann let her son Dan go to visit an expensive school three thousand miles from home. She knew she couldn't afford it even with a financial package. Naturally, Dan fell in love with the school and was devastated when told it was not an option. Ann's advice: "Don't even look at something you know is out of the question."

How many schools should you apply to? There's not one right answer, but consider five. It's smart to apply to one "safe" school where your teen has an excellent chance of acceptance and one "stretch" school that he'll be amazed to get into.

3. Investigate Fellowship

When you investigate a college, ask about fellowship. Campus Crusade, InterVarsity Christian Fellowship, and Fellowship of Christian Athletes can be found on most large secular campuses. There will likely be other groups as well. Get the name of a staff person and an involved student and phone or email them. Have them describe the fellowship.

Find out when it meets. Inquire about small Bible studies. Ask about churches near campus that have a vital college ministry. If you are considering Christian colleges, don't automatically assume they will be the answer for your child's faith. A Christian college could have an exciting fellowship group, or it could be a stilted legalistic atmosphere. Talking to current students or recent graduates can give you insights.

You will not be on campus to make your child attend church or fellowship. That will be his decision. Our job is that of a connector. An electrician determines the needs of a project. He collects his tools, and he lays out the wires that need to be connected. But the lights don't go on until the cord is plugged into the socket. That's the job of the homeowner. Our responsibility is much like this; we serve as a connector, but our child has to be the one who plugs in. We let him know where he can go for church and fellowship, and then pray that God will give him the desire to go once he's there.

There is no perfect campus, yet too often we do research to find the best fit for our child academically but fail to research the potential for spiritual growth. In the long run, it's spiritual growth that is the most crucial.

4. Visit the Schools

Visit the college with your child, especially if you've never seen the school. If possible, arrange ahead for your child to spend the night in a dorm with a believer. It's ideal to visit during the week on the night a campus fellowship meets. By attending the fellowship your child will be able to see if he can visualize himself as a part of that group. Encourage him to attend classes the next day. He will get a more realistic picture of college life midweek than on weekends. And if he chooses this particular school, he already will have met some believers.

It will relieve pressure if your child visits schools during his junior year. He will have a better idea of what he is interested in and he won't have to scramble during his senior year. If he can't visit every school he wants to apply to, he should apply anyway. He can always visit after being accepted. One of the reasons it is helpful to visit during the junior year is that more and more colleges are moving to "early decision" plans. These applications have to be in before or near the beginning of the senior year. Some are binding—if you are accepted, you pledge to attend. Therefore, if your child chooses to apply for early decision, he has to be sure of his first choice. If your child is borderline in his chances of being accepted, it can be to his advantage to apply for early decision. Each college admissions department will tell you their policy.

Schools vary widely on their personal interview policy. Some require one. Many say they won't give any. We have found that "no interview" doesn't necessarily mean "no interview." Be persistent. Large universities usually state that they give no interviews; however, alumni of the school can often arrange for a "personal conversation" with a school official. An informal, unofficial interview of this nature can play an important role in gaining admittance. It's prudent to explore this possibility.

As you visit each campus, you will adjust your criteria. Your child may decide he'd rather be in a small town than a big city. Part of the fun of having criteria to begin with is that they give us a starting point from which we can see our vision develop.

5. Finish the Application

"Don't you think you should finish your application?"

"How can you go out? You haven't done your college application, and it's due tomorrow!"

Nag, nag, nag.

We hate being the nag, and they don't like us very much either. We can alleviate being the nag if we discuss early—before it becomes an issue—target dates for having applications finished. The summer just prior to their senior year is a good time to get a start. If they are applying early decision, set the goal of having the application finished before school begins. It's wise to set the goal of Thanksgiving for all other applications to be finished. This will enable you to have a nag-free Christmas!

Ultimately it's their responsibility to get it done. Not ours. But planning ahead will make for a more pleasant atmosphere in the home.

I once sat on a parents' panel at the local public high school our kids all attended. Our job as panelists was to give advice to parents just beginning this college process. I became horrified as I listened to four of the five speakers before me discuss how they helped their teens fill out their applications and write their essays. When my turn came, I simply said, "I must respectfully disagree with my fellow panelists. Filling out applications is the child's responsibility. It's a matter of integrity. They are supposed to do it, not us."

Knowing some in the audience would not understand my view on integrity, I continued, "We will not be in college with them to write their papers for them. How can we expect them to be responsible in college if we don't give them responsibility while in high school?"

A few parents applauded. Others looked at me as if I were from the Dark Ages.

6. Make Your Decision

After your teen has heard from the colleges, you may still have some hard decisions to make. If she can't decide between two schools, consider having her make a second visit. Often being on the campus will give clarity.

Perhaps she got wait-listed or even rejected. If she really wants that particular school, pursue it further. Later it will be better to look back and feel that you did everything you could. If the final answer is still no, you will have the peace that God shut the door.

Keith was rejected at Berkeley, his first choice. A brilliant underachiever, his high school grades had not been up to the cut. Undaunted, he wrote the admissions office and appealed their decision. He was accepted upon further review.

Trevor was wait-listed at Princeton. He went back to Princeton and spoke to the people in admissions. He told them why he felt Princeton was the school for him. He was accepted.

Your teen may not get positive results like these boys did, but you don't lose anything by an appeal. It will give clarity to God's leading.

Too many choices can be confusing. "How do I know God's will? Where should I go? What if I make the wrong decision?"

Our son Chris and his friend Danny were confused. Time was running out. The deadline for responding to their acceptances was close. And they couldn't decide. We parents didn't know how to advise them either! Where was God leading them? None of us could see the answer.

The decision was overwhelming all of us. The pressure was intense.

Mimi came to the rescue. Mimi is Chris's grandmother and my mother. She has wisdom. And she brought relief!

"Boys," she said, "stop fretting so much. You aren't marrying the college. Pick one and go, and if it isn't right, you can transfer later."

Oh, the perspective that comes with age!

7. *Plan for the Adventure Ahead*

Once the decision is made, the next biggest issue is the roommate. Some teens want to room with someone they know, while others are eager to start fresh, meeting someone new. There are advantages to both. If your teen would like to room with someone they don't know, try to find a believer. Often through the network of believers, someone who knows someone, or someone's little sister you can find another student beginning at the same college. They don't have to become "best friends for life," and they may just live together for a year, but it makes a huge difference to begin college life living with someone with the same moral values. If your child simply takes potluck, she could end up with a roommate who has her boyfriend sleeping with her in their room, having sex in the bed right next to hers, or putting her in the awkward position of having to find someplace else to sleep. This is not a pressure your teen needs to deal with in her first few weeks of college. It might be better to match up with someone who has been recommended than to take a random choice.

Lots of people will offer your teen advice. Some you'll discard, and some will be valuable. When Chris went off to college at the University of North Carolina, we began a family tradition. We had a "celebrate Chris" send-off dinner. We gave him a photo collage of his family with love notes. And we took turns giving him advice. Allison and John had the best advice because they were already in college, but everyone had some tips. We continued this tradition with Susy and Libby. Some of our advice has included: Get to know one professor well and visit him outside of class; adopt a family at a church and spend time with them; spend time with different kinds of people; attend a fellowship meeting at least three times before deciding if it's the right one for you; wear a T-shirt that has a Christian logo on it on moving-in day and during the first few days—it will enable you to connect with other believers. Libby met a girl with a Young Life shirt on when we were unloading boxes to move into her dorm at the University of Virginia. It was such an encouragement to meet another believer so quickly on a large campus. One of the pieces of advice that Chris's dad gave him was, "Find an older girl who is a believer. Adopt her as your big sister. Spend time with her. Because she is older, it will be unlikely to be an awkward dating relationship. She will be an encouragement to you."

Chris took that advice and met a senior at a fellowship meeting. He asked if he could get together with her for coffee to get some advice. It was the beginning of a special friendship. She got him through some rough challenges his freshman year.

"Have realistic expectations," Allison warned Chris. "I was miserable first semester. I cried a lot because I was homesick. But at the end of second semester, I cried because I was sad to leave school and all my friends for the summer! Don't make judgments based on one semester."

8. Pray for the Details Ahead

Once the decision is made, the focus of our prayers changes from "Show us the place, God," to "Go before us and prepare the way."

When we gather for our yearly "needs and goals" sharing session with our teens, our college kids give us specific things to pray for.

A big prayer request has been for God to give each of our kids an older believer of the same sex to serve as a "spiritual mentor." One of the most encouraging things to me about this young generation is their longing for mentors. At UNC, Chris found Colin, a doctoral student. They began to meet together regularly for prayer, sharing, and study. When Chris had challenges, Colin provided encouragement and wise counsel. Spending time with Colin and his wife gave Chris a picture of a healthy young marriage.

Before he went off to college, Tyler asked his parents to pray that he wouldn't get too down if things weren't immediately what he hoped they'd be. Well, they weren't. He was lonely, had a roommate he didn't click with, and missed his family. But he hung in there, and in time God supplied Eric, another basketball lover who became a good friend.

Before Chris's friend Zach began his junior year in college, he wrote out his goals in four categories: spiritual, academic, physical, social. Some of his spiritual goals were: to get into the Word daily, to pray consistently for his parents and sister, Julie, and to look for opportunities to share Christ. One academic goal was to go to all classes and to participate! A physical goal was to lift weights three times a week with Joel. A social goal was to use meals as a time of fellowship.

Take some time as a family to share needs and goals for the coming year. If you haven't done this before, utilize sending a kid off to college as a natural time to introduce this concept. It's a way of staying connected and of praying for the one who is away. It's also a way of keeping him in touch with what's happening in his siblings' lives.

Our sons, John and Chris, recently published a book, *The Incredible Four-Year Adventure: Finding Real Faith, Fun, and Friendship at College.* It is full of stories from students at a variety of colleges, and it will be encouraging for high school students as they prepare for life after graduation.[1] It's also a good book for parents to read. You will gain a better understanding of today's college world.

April 1 came, and our daughter Susy got a thin letter. We all burst into tears. It was to have been the perfect college. The only place she wanted to go—UNC, to be with her brother Chris. She should have gotten in. But she didn't. God had a "better place" for her.

Midway through first semester we got an email from her at Miami of Ohio. It read, "I just wanted to tell you all that I am so happy here. I feel like I have been surrounded by fellowship since I've been here. Merrit (a junior) is so genuine, and I am so excited to have her disciple me. I know that the Lord has such a perfect plan for me. He knew I was supposed to be here, and I thank Him for loving me so much that although He had to make me sad and miserable when not getting into UNC, that there is even a better place. (Yes, Chris, a better place!) I am learning so much and feel the presence of the Lord so strongly here. I am grateful for all He is teaching me."

God knows what is best for your child. He *is* faithful and He *will* lead.

Focus Questions

Meditate on Joshua 1:1–9.

1. In this passage we see that Joshua is assuming his new responsibility as leader of the children of Israel. What words of instruction does God give to him in this new season? How do these words apply to you as you look forward to a new season with your teen?

2. What are special gifts and interests that you have observed in your teen? What are his special needs? What are his long-term dreams? As you consider the first year after high school, what options would best meet these needs?

3. If your child is a junior or senior, have a brainstorming session together. Discuss several different possibilities for his first year after graduation. Develop together a list of questions for which you will need answers. Decide who will find which answers. Let your child assume the major responsibility for this fact finding.

4. Using the ideas from this chapter as a sample, develop your own strategy for making a decision about which college or which job. If your child is not interested in these discussions, or if you are a single parent, it will be more fun and you will get a better response if you do this together with another family whose child matches yours in age. Keep in mind that each child is unique.

Meditate on Philippians 1:3–11. Use this as your prayer of blessing for your teen as he leaves.

> Be strong and courageous. Do not be terrified; do not be discouraged, for the LORD your God will be with you wherever you go.
>
> Joshua 1:9

11

Training in Life Skills and Letting Go

Leaving—is my child ready? Am I?

Our son Chris was nineteen and his brother, John, was twenty-one, but what they were proposing still scared me to death.

"Mom and Dad, we want to take two months this coming summer and bike across America with our buddies, Nate and Rob. We'd like to start in the Pacific Ocean and finish in the Atlantic Ocean. And we'd like your blessing."

Everything in me wanted to scream, *That's the craziest thing I've ever heard. What if a car hits you? What if some crazy person murders you on the side of the road? What if you get in trouble and can't get help? What if . . . !* Scary thoughts. And this wasn't just a fantasy. These boys were dead serious.

There were practical questions too. How would you stay in touch with us? How will you make enough money to finance this? How will you train for this and do well in school at the same time? Would you camp the whole way? When would you leave? What roads would you take? Do you know what you are doing? *I don't think so.*

We told the boys we would be willing to consider a detailed proposal when they had done more research. *Surely they'll change their minds once they look into it,* I tried to convince myself.

A month later, three sets of parents gathered in our family room to hear the boys present their case. They had done massive amounts of research, outlined the whole trip, raised and presented their answers to every question they thought we'd ask. Their research was given to us in a neatly prepared written proposal. And worst of all, they asked us to pray with them about this. I didn't want to pray. I just wanted to say no!

I had so many fears. So many "what-if's." There weren't any guarantees. It was a huge, unnecessary risk. I wouldn't be there. I would really have to let go and trust them and God. I was a lot surer of the God part than the boy part. Were they ready for something this big? Was I?

No matter when or where our kids go, it's hard. It's painful. After all, it's a frightening world out there. And we are no longer in control in the way we used to be.

How Do We Handle Their Leaving?

When Lib's daughter left for college, she missed her terribly. She called every day to touch base and discuss how things were going. She helped her daughter decide which classes to take, what to wear to a special function, how she should handle an awkward roommate situation. She monitored her sleep and made recommendations about which extracurricular activities to join. In short, she directed her daily schedule long-distance. When her daughter called in tears about a blowup with her roommate, Lib spent the day worrying and figuring out how to fix the situation. By evening when she talked to her daughter again, her daughter's response was, "Oh, Mom, that was no big deal; we're fine now."

Although Lib's intentions were only to be supportive, she was overparenting.

When Sarah's daughter left for college, her mother breathed a sigh of relief. "She's on her own now. She'll either sink or swim." When they talked on the phone, which was rare, she simply asked how things were going. When her daughter decided she didn't like her roommate and moved off campus into an expensive apartment, Sarah simply said, "It's your decision." When her daughter began to show signs of an eating disorder, Sarah's response was, "She has to deal with this in her own way. It's not my responsibility any more." Although Sarah's intentions were to give her child freedom in the hopes that she would grow up, she was letting go too abruptly.

Sarah and Lib represent two extremes in parenting: *overparenting* and *abdicating*. Usually we will tend toward one or the other. Recognize your tendency and seek to achieve balance. But remember, it will be very awkward for each of us because it's a new season.

How Do We Maintain Balance?

Recognize That Independence Is Gradual, Not Sudden

We may have the attitude that when they graduate from high school and leave home—"Boom, they're on their own.

My nest is now empty!" Our experience and that of many others has been that the nest isn't really empty. It's more of a "Bungee Cord Season" than an "Empty Nest Season"—they bounce back! I don't think the "empty nest" really begins until they graduate from college and begin their own careers or marry. If they are in college, they have vacations and come home bringing friends, dirty laundry, empty stomachs, and sleep-deprived bodies. As we discussed in the preceding chapter, high school graduates are usually seventeen or eighteen. They are still underage and usually financially dependent upon their parents, at least to some degree. Their first year out will be the hardest. We have to guard against the extreme that says, *When they leave home we are no longer responsible, nor should we interfere.*

Instead, we need to let them go in stages. Just because they are gone, they aren't instantly making all of their own decisions. Yes, they do need to make more and more of their own decisions. And yes, they will make some poor ones. They will learn from their mistakes. But "out of the nest and into college" doesn't mean our responsibility is over.

Let Go of the Right Things

Lib needed to let go of the daily details of her daughter's life. Her daughter needed to decide on her classes, what to wear, how to handle normal relationship problems. When her daughter called for advice, Lib learned how to say, "Sweetie, that's a decision you have to make. I'll pray for wisdom." When we turn over decision making to our kids, they will grow in personal confidence. If we have been doing this in stages while they were at home, this transition will be easier.

Sarah needed to be more involved in her daughter's life. An eating disorder can be life threatening. Parental involvement is necessary. Large financial decisions should be made *jointly*. After all, as parents you are probably paying some of the bills. Academics is another area in which the parents should be involved. Skipping classes repeatedly and partying all weekend may impact a semester's grades. If this is the case by the semester's end, it's time to get involved. Moral issues and safety issues also require parental involvement.

Kem and Norma have had five teens. When their kids became teenagers, they challenged each one to make a pledge not to drink or smoke until they were twenty-one. They promised each of them a financial reward if they were able to keep this pledge completely. They knew their kids would be honest with them. Yes, it was hard for the kids. When the fraternity boys tried to get their son to drink, he told them of the pledge he'd made his folks. Although they kidded him, they also let him know that they respected him. In time his actions became a testimony to other collegians: You can be a believer living out your convictions and still have fun.

How you make decisions with your teen is going to depend upon your unique relationship with him and your history of communication. There is not one right way. But if you skipped to this chapter for a quick formula for "letting go," go back and read the preceding chapters. How you adjust to this season of change will be directly impacted by what has gone on before.

Expect Awkwardness and Some Tension

"Son, I just want you to know that this is a new season not only for you as you leave, but for us as your parents. You may want more freedom than we are ready to give—or you may wonder if the infrequency of our phone calls means that we don't care! We will have to work extra hard in communicating honestly with each other during this exciting new season. And we have to be patient with one another when we make mistakes."

In this new season, that old jigsaw puzzle of a family unit has been tossed into the air once again. Now we have to learn how best to relate to an independent child. This may cause some tension in your marriage, especially if you each lean toward a different extreme.

Peg worried about every detail of Justin's life. When she moved him into the dorm, she took all her cleaning equipment to scrub his room and to disinfect every drawer. She arranged to get his dirty clothes home so she could do his laundry. When he struggled in a course, she drove to his school to help him study. Her husband pleaded with her to let the boy go. "I'm just trying to help. He needs me," was her reply. Not surprisingly, tension developed in their marriage. Listen to your mate. Ask, "Am I too involved, or have I abdicated things I should not?" Talk with a couple whose experience with older children has been good. Learn from them.

We see what can happen if we overparent or if we abdicate too much too fast. Anticipating what lies ahead can enable us to better prepare for this transition season.

How Do We Prepare Them for Leaving?

If we have been "letting go" all along, we will have a much easier adjustment in this new season. If our child has already learned basic life skills, we will be less likely to interfere in the details of her daily life, and we will have prepared her for living in the world. Our role is to equip our kids with life skills. This requires intentional training. If we don't train them, we unintentionally handicap them in the guise of serving them by doing things for them that they should be doing themselves. Training in life skills begins early. It's training in responsibility, in independence. This sense of responsibility breeds confidence. Our teens are going to have enough new adjustments in the world without having to learn skills they could have learned at home.

Here are eleven brief life skills to teach your kids. You will want to add to this list yourself, so consider this a starting place. The earlier you begin this training, the better!

1. Teach Them Good Manners

Teach your kids proper table manners. Keep arms and elbows off the table. Sit up straight. Put your napkin in your lap. Leave your fork and knife together when finished. Ask to be excused before leaving the table. Show them how to set a proper table and which utensils to use for what. If you don't know, check out a book on table settings from your library. This may seem silly in an increasingly casual society and in a family dealing with teens who have more crucial issues, but it's important. Why? Our job as parents is to equip our kids so that they will know how to behave in whatever place God chooses to put them.

I want my kids to be comfortable dining at the White House or with kings and princesses. And I want them to be comfortable in a simple pauper's hut. We do not want our kids to be embarrassed because they don't know how to act. We do not know where God will call them. That's His job. Our job is to equip them to be able to behave properly in whatever places God puts them, and to know how to honor their host or hostess. Using proper manners is a way of paying respect, of communicating honor to another person. Our kids will not simply pick this up. It has to be specifically taught.

When our kids were young, we occasionally pretended we were dining at the White House. We used good china, linen napkins, lots of utensils, and we practiced good manners. I made it as much of a game as I could. No, my kids don't have perfect manners. And my husband still tells me to take my elbows off the table! But we are trying.

My friend Peggy, a professional protocol consultant, says that the single biggest irritant transcending all nationalities is the failure to RSVP. Usually the request is simply ignored. We have to realize that this can be costly to a hostess who is being billed per head. It can also mess up seating arrangements. If you RSVP, it is important to show up! We need to teach our children that if there is a last-minute emergency, it is proper to call and offer their regrets.

There are lots of other manners we need to teach. Some of ours include: Stand up when a lady enters the room. Greet your family members and guests at the door when they arrive. Walk your guests to the door when they leave. Offer to help with the dishes. Open doors for others. Walk your dates to the door. And don't honk when you pick them up! Make your own family list of "good manners."

2. Teach Them to Write Thank-You Notes

If you read Ann Landers's column, you will notice that her letters most often fall into two categories: letters from people in pain over affairs and letters from grandparents in pain because they never receive thank-you notes from their grandchildren.

Thank-you notes should be written for any gifts received. Teach your kids to write a thank-you note when someone takes them out to dinner or does anything out of the ordinary for them. Train them to write a thank-you note to the parents of friends they visit out of town or to thank someone for the use of a house or car. When in doubt, instruct them to simply write a note. It is always appreciated. It is a way of honoring and loving someone. It is a positive testimony.

Post a date after Christmas or a birthday by which all thank-you notes must be finished. The use of the car, TV, or computer is prohibited after the deadline, unless notes are finished. If you do this while your kids are at home, they'll be more likely to follow through when they leave home. But you may have to remind them during that first year away. A graduation gift of nice stationery will encourage this habit.

3. Teach Them How to Be Good Guests

Over the years that our college kids have brought friends home, I have received some of the dearest thank-you notes from these guests. I've saved many of these notes. They are a tribute to wise parents.

Being a good guest means writing a thank-you note, but it also means other things. Teach your teens to take a hostess gift. Give them suggestions. Our son Chris went to college a half hour from his grandmother. "Son," I suggested, "whenever you go see Grandmother, take her some flowers." When John went to visit his girlfriend's parents, I helped him fix a basket of jams and jellies to take.

A good guest offers to help with the meal preparation and cleanup. A good guest makes his bed, hangs up the towels in the bathroom, and leaves his room neat. If teens are using someone's cabin or car, teach them to leave it clean. The owners will appreciate it. And the teens will more likely be invited back.

A good guest sits with adults and talks to them. He looks them in the eye. This takes lots of practice in the home. Help your child think up good questions to ask. Questions like, "What do you enjoy the most in your job? What are you looking forward to in the next several months? What advice would you give to someone my age? Who is someone who has had a positive impact on your life? Why do you admire this person?" Develop your own list of good conversation questions.

If your child has a collection of "good conversation starters," he will be more at ease in communicating with adults. Include him in adult conversations with your friends at home. Clue him in about the adults coming to dinner. Give him suggestions of things he might talk to a specific adult about. What are this adult's interests? What questions might he ask the adult? The dinner table is a great training ground. But don't expect instant results. It will take years of doing this at home to prepare him to be able to communicate comfortably with adults when he leaves.

How do we teach this without making life miserable? Declare a "good guest–bad guest night." Divide into two teams and produce two skits each—one depicting a good guest and the other a bad guest. Depending upon the ages of your kids, you can add crazy costumes for fun or see who can produce the best and worst conversations. Several families can do this together. We have to do what we can to make training in life skills fun, while at the same time realizing that it won't be all fun and it won't be all learned at once. It takes years of repetition, and we are unlikely to see the results until the late teen years.

4. Teach Them to Clean Up

Doug went off to college with high standards. His faith was strong, and he had a vision for making a difference for Christ on his campus. Midway though his college years, one of the other guys in his apartment came to him and said, "Doug, we've asked you many times to clean up your messes, but you haven't. You are always leaving your dirty dishes out for someone else to wash. Your smelly clothes are left all over the apartment, and we've had it. You are self-centered, and you need to deal with this." It was a painful confrontation for a good guy who was trying to be a witness. And it could have been avoided.

Doug had grown up in a happily messy home. His mom considered herself a "Messie" and was lax in training her children to pick up. *He is so busy and under so much pressure,* she reasoned. *I don't want to make him pick up too. Besides, it's just the way he is. It's his personality.*

His messiness may well have been due to his personality type. Some of us err on the side of messy and some on the side of compulsive neatness, which is also unnerving. But it's not the personality trait that is at issue here. It's the character trait. The character trait in question is that of thoughtfulness. It is not thoughtful to your roommates to leave your mess all around. It is not considerate of your future spouse to make a mess and leave it. We are training future roommates, husbands, and wives in thoughtfulness. Teaching them the skill of cleaning up their mess is training in character. Have a chore chart in your home. Set times for the chores to be done and the house to be picked up. Follow through. A conflict like Doug's is one our child will be less likely to have to deal with when he leaves home if we have had standards of cleanliness and followed through on them in our own home, even if that isn't our personality.

5. Teach Them to Do Their Own Laundry

Ellen was really concerned about her son. He'd been gone several months already, and she was sure he hadn't done his wash. So she kept sending him care packages of boxer shorts! By the time he came home for a visit, she'd already mailed him seventeen pairs of boxers in addition to what he took to school!

Steve called his mom the first week of school in a panic. His favorite shirt was the size of a little girl's. What had happened? All he'd done was wash it and dry it on hot.

Our kids have enough adjustments to make without having to cope with learning to do their own laundry for the first time.

Turn the laundry over to them by the time they reach high school. It'll be one less adjustment later, and it'll keep you from overparenting. I discovered my kids could do their own laundry when I accidentally turned all of my son's T-shirts pink.

"Mom, please don't do any more of my laundry! I'd rather do it myself."

He didn't trust me with his laundry. Wonderful!

I bought five different-colored laundry baskets, one for each child, and when they began high school they assumed the privilege of doing their own laundry. It was washed, dried, and then emptied by them into their basket. Rarely did it make it into their dressers. And it didn't get ironed until they needed to iron it to wear. But they learned how to do their own laundry!

6. Teach Them to Remember Birthdays

Beth is a single parent with three sons. The first year after her separation, her birthday came and went, and none of her teenage sons remembered it. Not only were her feelings hurt, but she also realized that there was a bigger issue here. She was raising future husbands who would need to know how to pamper their wives on their birthdays. So she sat her boys down and explained to them how their forgetfulness had hurt her. She talked with them about how women need to be treated and gave them specific suggestions for what they could do for future birthdays, Mother's Day, and Christmas. The next year she humorously reminded them. She said, "Hey, guys, what happens in ten days?" The following day she said, "Hey, guys, what happens in nine days?" She also gave them a long list of suggestions for gifts. This basic life skill will help them in the future.

Many of us buy gifts for our kids to give to others. We must begin to turn this responsibility over to them during the teen years, before they leave home. Give them a list of dates to remember. Include their grandparents' birthdays on it. Help them begin to budget to pay for the gifts or cards themselves. Give them suggestions for a gift or card, but let them buy it and mail it. If they learn this before they leave home, they will be more likely to follow through later, and they will have assumed another responsibility that will help them in either single or married life. When they leave for college, give them a card or calendar with important birthdays, addresses, and emails written on it. Be prepared to remind them that first year. But don't do it for them.

7. Give Them Basic Medical Knowledge

Do I go to the doctor or not? Am I really sick or just tired? What medicine do I take for this? Can I take my roommate's medicine? These questions can be difficult to answer and frustrating for the parent miles away. Begin *now* to teach your child basic first aid. Prepare a first-aid kit for him. Include Tylenol or ibuprofen, Nyquil or something similar for flu symptoms, Neosporin for cuts, an antihistamine for allergies, cortisone cream for bites, yule cream for poison ivy, Pepto-Bismol for an upset stomach, a thermometer, an ice pack, and plenty of Band-Aids! Warn him against sharing his friends' prescription drugs. Be sure he knows what to use when. Make sure he has your insurance information and knows how to use it.

When in doubt tell your kids to go to the student health center. Mononucleosis is rampant on college campuses, and if your teen is sick for over a week, he should see a physician.

8. Teach Them to Manage Their Own Finances

Much of this we covered in the "Hot Topics" chapter, but it has to be mentioned again because money can be a tremendous source of tension if the skills of handling it have not been taught.

Dy Vest, a young student, owns two T-shirts that he says cost him $2,500. He got the shirts for free when he signed up for two credit cards at the campus center during freshman orientation. Within a year he had bills of $2,500 that he could not pay. Later he had to drop out of school for a semester to pay off his credit card bills. Now he's been debt-free for two years.

According to national studies, between 55 and 70 percent of college students own at least one credit card. Between a third and a half of these students don't pay their monthly credit card bills in full. On today's campuses it's almost impossible to avoid credit card pitches. Easy applications are found in orientation gift bags, hanging on bulletin boards, and in the mail.[1] Wise parents will determine their credit card policy before their teen leaves home. A credit card should always be paid off in full before the due date.

Before your child leaves home, draw up a proposed budget that includes what expenses are his responsibility and what are yours. For example, who is going to pay for his phone calls? Our policy has been that our kids pay for all calls they make to anyone other than family members. I pay for calls home and to siblings and grandparents. I want to encourage these relationships, and my paying for these calls makes it easier for them to call a brother or sister. As you work these issues out, insist that your teen write down where every penny goes the first semester. It may help to give him a financial record notebook and together create categories of anticipated expenses.

He may be shocked to discover just how much of his semester's money goes for late-night pizza. She may be astounded at how much her own phone bill is. During semester break go over these records and make adjustments for second semester. Plan to discuss together any major expenses—

before they are incurred—during this first year. There will be adjustments. You will have expenses you did not anticipate, so plan for a cushion.

9. Teach Them to Make and Keep Their Own Appointments

"Mrs. _____, your son was supposed to come in today to have his teeth cleaned, and he hasn't shown up yet. We are calling to find out where he is," the message on the machine repeats.

With a huge groan, you slump into a chair. *He forgot again. I forgot to remind him. I can't remember everything. I have too many other things to keep up with. And when I try to schedule his appointments, it always seems to interfere with his life, and he gets irritated. What am I going to do?*

Whoa. Call a halt. Why are you scheduling his appointments, anyway? It's a life skill he needs to be responsible for before he ever leaves home. By his sophomore year he should be responsible for making and keeping his own appointments for the dentist, doctor, and the like. Yes, he needs to clear the date with you and arrange for transportation, but that's his responsibility. Many doctors charge a fee if the appointment is not canceled twenty-four hours prior to the visit. If he forgets, the fee is his responsibility. (Okay, if he's usually responsible and forgets one time, grant him grace and pay the fee, but just this once.)

A larger issue is at stake here, as in almost every one of these life skills. It's time management. Your teen knows his own schedule best, and he must learn how to fit necessary appointments into his busy life. If you do it for him, you are only going to make it harder for him to control his life when he leaves home.

Teach him how to use the yellow pages. Sure he can dial information, but it costs extra. Where is the best repair shop for his guitar? Who has the most competitive prices for software? What about auto repairs? What bank offers the best account for his needs? Let your teens begin to do such necessary research while they are in high school. A complex society has lots of details that can be a nuisance. If your teen learns how to handle these while he is at home, he will have a more realistic picture of what real life is about and one less adjustment to make when he leaves home.

10. Teach Them Basic Auto Mechanics

Both Johnny and I are hopelessly unmechanical. Even though my dad made me change a tire twice before he let me get my license, I still don't know what line is positive and what is negative on the battery. Johnny is just a little bit better than I am, but thank goodness we have Jerry! Our friend and neighbor, he knows everything about cars. When our boys were teens, Johnny asked him to teach them basic auto mechanics. Jerry showed them how to check the belts, when to change the hoses, fill the radiator, and much more.

Basic automobile knowledge is a life skill all our kids need, both boys and girls, even if they don't have a car themselves. One day they will own a car, and they may occasionally drive a friend's car on campus.

Before they go, they need to know how to check and add oil and other fluids, how to change a flat tire, how to recharge a dead battery, how to drive manual in addition to automatic transmission (in an emergency they may have to drive either), how to spot unevenly wearing tires, and how to handle other basic repairs.

If you don't have this knowledge yourself, organize one special Saturday morning "Auto Mechanics Class" at your church and ask a member who does know to teach the teens (and the parents who need it!).

In addition, be sure your teen knows your insurance policy, and when and how to get your car inspected. Have him take your car in for the next inspection. Explain what to do in case of an accident. Remind him that if he borrows a car, he should return it clean, with a full tank of gas.

11. Teach Basic Meal Planning

Our son Chris went off to college with a rice cooker and a tight budget. First semester he signed up for too many activities, slept too little, lived on rice and pb&j sandwiches, and came home at Christmas with mono. It was a painful lesson in nutrition and time management!

An understanding of good eating habits begins at home. With the rise in eating disorders, an understanding of nutrition is particularly important. Encourage your schools to teach nutrition as a part of their health unit. Challenge your teens to do a paper on nutrition for a class. If you home school, teach a unit on basic nutrition. Practice good eating habits yourself. Give each of your teens a simple cookbook. Assign two siblings one special night to cook. Give them several days' notice. Have them do the meal planning and the shopping. Show them how to clip coupons to save money. Be sure you praise them for their meal even if it isn't your favorite dish.

When we go on family vacations, we divide up the cooking and cleaning responsibilities. It's the only way I get a break! This tradition has evolved into a family cook-off. Each evening two different people are paired up to do the cooking. They plan the menu, do the shopping, prepare the meal, and clean up. I pay for the food. Over the years, the kids have developed their own specialties. This summer Chris and his wife, Christy, made crab cakes, fresh corn, and an exotic salad. He's come a long way from rice and pb&j sandwiches!

Okay, by now you are either feeling pretty good about your parenting, or you are a bit panicked. *My child's a senior. I have to teach it all this year!* This is one sure way to make your life and his miserable. Balance is needed. You do not have to make your child perfect before he leaves home. On the other hand, if you've been doing most things for him, you definitely need to let up and turn more over to him.

I took a walk recently with my friend Barbara. Her son is going into his senior year. All of a sudden it has hit her that she has so little time to "finish" with this child.

"Susan," she said, "I feel like I'm always on his back. I'm such a perfectionist, and I want to make sure he knows everything he needs to before he leaves. He still has so many rough edges. But I sense he's resenting me. Our relationship is not comfortable."

"You've done a great job with this son," I responded. "He's got a strong faith. He's a leader in school and at church. He's conscientious, and he's a good boy. Quit trying to make him perfect in this last year. Instead, ENJOY him. Thank God each day for one trait that you appreciate in him, and then tell him from time to time what you appreciate about him. Spend time with him once a week with no agenda. Hang out simply to be with him. Go for a walk together. Go get ice cream. He may not respond because he'll suspect you have an agenda—but persist. Over time he will warm up, and you will have spent your last year with him building a friendship instead of trying to make him perfect."

Now, what about you? Are you ready for your teen to leave?

On a good day you don't want her to leave. On a bad day you can't wait for her to leave!

You will vacillate in your emotions. So will she. That's normal. But you need to take time to get yourself ready, especially if you are the mom.

A wise woman will begin to prepare for life after kids before they ever leave. Take a class, go back to school, investigate a new career. If you've been at home full-time, this is particularly important. It will be far easier on you and on your teen if you have something meaningful to occupy your time when she is gone. You will be far less likely to overparent.

It's important for Dad to encourage Mom in this new endeavor. Her gifts and talents may have been on hold for some time. She needs positive encouragement as she seeks a fresh focus. Understand that a child's leaving will likely have a greater impact on Mom than on Dad. Change can cause dissension in a marriage. Talk about the changes ahead of you before they happen. Share your hopes and fears with one another. Determine specific things you will do to grow closer during this time as a couple. Specific plans will protect you from drifting apart in this new season.

Our boys did bike across America. Chris, Rob, and Nate began with their feet in the Pacific Ocean at Canon Beach, Oregon. John joined them in Kansas, and sixty days after takeoff they peddled sunburned, tired, lean bodies through a large banner into a crowd of family, friends, and press—and into the waves of the Atlantic Ocean on the coast of Virginia Beach.

Two months full of incredible adventures—illness, accidents, extraordinary kindness from strangers, amusing encounters with local characters, spiritual growth, and yes, an advanced course in life skills.

For me it was a painful summer of letting go. Of staying in Psalm 91 and on my knees in prayer. Of relying on God's faithfulness in a new way. It wasn't easy. But letting go is never easy.

It wasn't easy for God to let go of His Son and send Him to this earth where He would be misunderstood, ridiculed, hated, and finally crucified. And yet He did it out of His incredible love for you and for me. He understands how we feel as we enter this season of letting our child go. He is a parent too.

But wait! There is also joy in letting go! We see that our kids have learned some life skills after all. Their confidence has grown. They've accomplished something new. Yes, there have been failures, but they've pressed on. And in this process God has again taught their parents that these children belong to Him. In letting go, we are simply giving them again into the hand of the One who loves them even more than we do.

Focus Questions

Meditate on Psalm 91.

1. How does this psalm encourage you as you let your child go?

2. Would you say that you tend to overparent or to abdicate too quickly? What can you do to become more balanced?

3. Discuss with your spouse (or another couple) some of the life skills you want to teach your child. Include the age you want to begin the training and two or three ways you will accomplish it.

4. What steps do you need to take as a couple or individually to prepare yourself for your teen's leaving?

5. What can you do to give your child a blessing as he leaves?

Meditate on 1 Corinthians 1:8 and 2 Timothy 1:12. Use a concordance to look up related verses about God's faithfulness. Write a letter to God thanking Him for specific ways He has been faithful to you and to your teens.

> He who dwells in the shelter of the Most High
>   will rest in the shadow of the Almighty.
> I will say of the LORD, "He is my refuge and my
>   fortress,
>   my God, in whom I trust."
>
> Psalm 91:1–2

Epilogue

At the Window Again

Once again I was at my front window. This time I watched as Susy and Libby threw their arms around each other and burst into tears.

Twenty of us had just spent a wonderful Easter weekend together. Our kids had brought friends home from college for the holiday. Most of them were freshmen, experiencing their first time away from home. We'd had a great slumber party at our farm, a giant biblical trivia scavenger hunt between "Team Michigan" and "Team Virginia." (Team Virginia won when they found the answer in the Bible to, "Who was the man who ran away naked?") We had sung along with guitars, shared lessons from the year at school, and danced on the old porch. We had attended a wonderful worship service at church on Sunday and had a formal Easter dinner in our front yard!

But now it was time to go, and leaving was so hard. The twins had been apart for the first time this year, and this reunion had been so sweet. But it was over, good-byes had to be said, and the tears flowed freely.

As I watched the girls, my eyes also filled with tears. Tears of joy and tears of sadness. Joy for kids who love each other, joy for their friends who love Christ, joy for this season of teenagers. But there were also tears of sadness. My "babies" were leaving. My nest was emptying out, albeit temporarily. I knew they would be back with more friends and more dirty laundry. But it was the beginning of a new season.

A new season. A season of letting go even more. A season of realizing again and again that I can't "fix things" for them. A season of breakups and start-ups. A season with four kids "in love" at the same time. A season of deepening friendships with adult children. A season with more time for Johnny and me to be together. A season of learning to trust God in new ways.

With this new season comes a deep sense of thanksgiving. I am thankful that God is bigger than the mistakes I've made in parenting. Thankful that He knows that I am but dust. Thankful that His strength is perfected in my weakness. Thankful that there is nothing He can't redeem. Thankful that nothing is impossible for Him. Thankful that He loves my kids even more than I do, and that He has a plan for each one of them. Thankful that He also has a plan for me in this new season, as my parenting responsibilities decrease.

Now, I wait at the window for my grandchildren—longing to watch their little feet pound up the walk, waiting to hear them shout, "Ghee and Poppy, here we are!"

What incredible joy.

Resources

For Help in Training Teens in Money Management

Get a Grip on Your Money: A Young Adult Study in Christian Financial Management by Larry Burkett, Focus on the Family Publishing, 1990.

For Help with Crisis Pregnancy

America's Crisis Pregnancy Helpline: 1-800-672-2296
National Life Center: 1-800-848-LOVE
Carenet: 1-800-395-4357
Birth Mothers: 1-877-77BIRTH, www.birthmothers.org

For Postabortion Help

Ramah International: 941-473-2188
www.ramahinternational.org

For Information on Cults

The Spiritual Counterfeits Project, Berkley, California, Danny Aguirre, Director. 510-540-5767, www.scp-inc. org

For Help with Pornography Addictions

National Coalition for Protection of Children and Families: 1-800-583-2964

Christian Camps

(This is not a complete list. It is simply the ones with which we are familiar.)

Focus Conferences: a ministry for private school kids.
    508-693-4824
    www.Infocus.org
    Martha's Vineyard, Massachusetts

Young Life: camps for high school kids across the country.
    719-381-1800
    www.younglife.org
    Nationwide

Kanakuk-Kanakomo: a Christian athletic camp; they also have a camp for special needs kids.
    417-334-2432
    www.kanakuk.com
    Branson, Missouri area

Summer's Best Two Weeks (SB2W): A Christian camp committed to using sports and outdoor adventure to reach today's kids.
814-629-9744
www.sb2w.org
Pennsylvania

Fellowship of Christian Athletes:
816-921-0909
www.FCA.org
Nationwide

Hume Lake Christian Camps:
559-251-6043
www.humelake.org
California

Spring Hill Camps:
www.springhillcamps.com
Michigan

Camp Timberline:
970-484-8462
www.camptimberline.com
Colorado

Brookwoods and Deer Run:
603-875-3600
www.brookwoods.org
New Hampshire

Notes

Chapter 3: Creating an Atmosphere of Encouragement

1. John and Susan Yates, *Character Matters! Raising Kids with Values That Last* (Grand Rapids: Baker, 2002).

2. Mark Stewart, "Full Plates," *The Washington Times*, 14 September 1999, sec. E, p. 3.

Chapter 4: Building Good Communication

1. This chart comes from Family Life's Marriage Conference Manual. Used by permission. Family Life is a ministry of Campus Crusade for Christ. Contact 1-800-FLTODAY or www.familylife.com.

Chapter 6: Handling the "Hot Topics"

1. Contact Exodus International, P.O. Box 2121, San Rafael, CA 94912; 415-454-1017. Exodus is an umbrella organization of over two hundred ministries worldwide that treat homosexuality from a variety of Christian perspectives. It offers referrals and additional resources.

2. This translation is taken from the NEW AMERICAN STANDARD BIBLE®. Copyright © The Lockman Foundation 1960, 1962, 1963, 1968, 1971, 1972, 1973, 1975, 1977, 1995. Used by permission.

3. Contact Focus on the Family, 1-800-AFAMILY, to order this resource, "Preparing for Adolescence." Check out their website: www.family.org.

4. Contact Family Life Today, 1-800-FLTODAY, to order this resource, "Passport to Purity."

5. We ordered the key and heart charms from the Focus on the Family Resource Center, 1-800-AFAMILY. Most jewelry stores will have gold necklaces.

6. Purity Covenant from the Marriage Conference Manual of Family Life, a ministry of Campus Crusade for Christ.

7. For the *Let's Talk about It* video, contact Ash and Eva Ashburn at Young Life and Gospel Seed offices, 1-800-341-9902.

8. "Alcoholism Affects 1 in 4 Children," *The Washington Post*, 2 January 2000, sec. A, p. 5.

9. You can find your local number for Alcoholics Anonymous in your phone book. Their web address is www.alcoholics-anonymous.org.

Al-Anon (for spouses of alcoholics) and Al-Ateen (for children of alcoholics) may be found by dialing 1-888-4AL-ANON. Their web address is www.al-anon.alateen.org.

10. Marc Kaufman, "Many Trying Tobacco in Grades 6–9," *The Washington Post*, 28 January 2000, sec. A, p. 16.

11. Eugene Peterson, *Like Dew Your Youth* (Grand Rapids: Eerdmans, 1976), 92.

12. To order a catalog, call Gateway Films at 1-800-523-0226.

Chapter 7: Taking Advantage of Peer Pressure

1. Wynne Wasson, "75 Will Face Party Charges," *Richmond Times Dispatch*, 4 June 1999, sec. B, p. 1.

Chapter 8: Encouraging Your Teen's Faith

1. Catherine Edwards, "Wicca Casts Spell on Teen-Age Girls," *Insight*, 25 October 1999, 22–25.

2. Susan A. Yates, *How to Like the Ones You Love* (Grand Rapids: Baker, 2000), 88–90.

Chapter 9: Finding Hope When Things Don't Turn Out

1. Some of the truths Christie began to dwell on include:
   I am accepted and worthy (Psalm 139; Rom. 15:7).
   I am never alone (Rom. 8:38–39; Heb. 13:5b).
   God will be faithful to me (Phil. 1:6; 2:13; 2 Thess. 3:3).
   I have hope (Pss. 16:11; 27:13; Rom. 15:13).
   I am seen as perfect (Col. 2:13; Heb. 10:14).
   I lack nothing (Phil. 4:19).

I am free from fear (Ps. 34:4; 2 Tim. 1:7).

I have strength (Ps. 37:39; Dan. 11:32).

I am victorious (Rom. 8:37; 2 Cor. 2:14).

I am protected (Ps. 32:7).

I have wisdom (Prov. 2:6, 7; 1 Cor. 1:30).

I have comfort (John 15:6; 16:7; 2 Cor. 1:3–4).

I am perfectly loved (John 15:9; Rom. 8:38–39).

I am totally forgiven (Ps. 103:12; Eph. 1:7; Heb. 10:17).

I have been declared righteous (Rom. 3:24; 1 Cor. 1:30).

I am indwelt by the Holy Spirit (Eph. 1:17–19).

I have direct access to God (Eph. 2:6; 1 Peter 2:5, 9).

I am blameless (John 3:18; Rom. 8:1).

I have been created for good works (Ps. 37:23; Eph. 2:10).

I am a new creation (2 Cor. 5:17).

I have authority over Satan (Col. 1:13; 1 John 4:4).

I have an eternal inheritance (Rom. 8:16–17; Eph. 1:11, 14, 18).

I have been raised with Christ (Rom. 6:4–8).

I will be with Christ in heaven (Eph. 2:5).

I have eternal security (1 John 5:11–13).

I have spiritual gifts for His service (1 Cor. 12).

2. Peterson, *Like Dew Your Youth*, 107.

3. For information on "You're Not Alone" conferences, go to www.notalone.org or call 489-752-8994.

Chapter 10: Helping Teens Choose the Right College or Job

1. John Yates and Chris Yates, *The Incredible Four-Year Adventure: Finding Real Faith, Fun, and Friendship at College* (Grand Rapids: Baker, 2000).

Chapter 11: Training in Life Skills and Letting Go

1. Liz Seymour, "College Credit Cards Increasing," *The Washington Post*, 1 November 1999, sec. B, p. 1.

Susan Alexander Yates is an accomplished author, magazine columnist for *Today's Christian Woman,* regular guest on radio programs, and a much-in-demand speaker on family life. She is well respected for her lighthearted yet instructive perspective on the challenges families face in an increasingly secular world. She is married to John Yates, Rector of The Falls Church, Episcopal. They have five children and two grandchildren and live in Falls Church, Virginia.